# God's Instruments for War

## Discovering and Coordinating Spiritual Gifts as Weapons of Warfare

Mike & Sue Dowgiewicz

Printed in the United States of America

ISBN 1-890592-06-4



**RESTORATION MINISTRIES**

*Equipping the Church to Go Back for Its Future*

**205 N. Murray Blvd, #[illegible] 25**
**Colorado Springs, CO 80916**
**719-573-4911**
**email:** mikedowg@aol.com
**www.restorationministries.org**

See back page for available materials.

# CONTENTS

# Introduction

"When did the Church begin? At Mount Sinai, when God chose to establish a relationship with the Jewish people." This answer was aptly shared by Dr. Howard Morgan of Restoration Foundation at the Open Church National Conference in Atlanta in September 1997. Think about the implications of our understanding of the Church if it began at Mt. Sinai when God separated out a people for Himself. The Church could learn much from God's interaction with, and purposes for, the Jewish people.

As more and more Christians let go of anti-Semitic lies about the irrelevancy of the Hebrew Bible (Old Testament), they are realizing that God is restoring the Hebraic roots of the Church. They are seeing God's relationship with man from God's vantage point, rather than from the man-centered view introduced into the Church by the converted Greek philosophers of the second and third centuries. The entire Bible shows a loving, caring Father's covenant relationship with His people. To view the Church apart from the Bible's testimony of God's motives and interactions in prior covenants does the Church a great disservice.

The Ten Commandments given at Mt. Sinai tell us that God wants His people to love Him. In return He promises to be merciful to a thousand generations. Because He *is* God, He has the right to stipulate our responsibilities in this relationship, such as honoring our parents, not stealing or coveting, caring for those who can never repay us. Failure to love and ignorance of His righteous purposes rob many believers of the fullness of being a child of a wonderful, caring Father.

Building on this understanding of loving God and fulfilling His purposes Paul writes, *"And we know that in all things God works for the good of those **who love him**, who have been **called according to his purpose**"* (Romans 8:28, emphasis added). As a people of destiny, followers of Jesus must first and foremost cling to a loving obedience that clearly hears and responds to the Master's call to arms.

The Israelites who sought to live out God's purposes were frequently faced with war. If they were going to inhabit the land of milk and honey—the Promised Land—they would have to fight for it. There could be no thought of compromise with the enemy:

*When the Lord your God brings you into the land you are entering to possess and drives out before you many nations—the Hittites, Girgashites, Amorites, Canaanites, Perizzites, Hivites and Jebusites, seven nations larger and stronger than you—and when the Lord your God has delivered them over to you and you have defeated them, then you must destroy them totally.* ***Make no treaty with them****, and show them no mercy. Do not intermarry with them. Do not give your daughters to their sons or take their daughters for your sons, for they will turn your sons away from following me to serve other gods, and the Lord's anger will burn against you and will quickly destroy you. This is what you are to do to them: Break down their altars, smash their sacred stones, cut down their Asherah poles and burn their idols in the fire.* ***For you are a people holy to the Lord your God.**** *The Lord your God has chosen you out of all the peoples on the face of the earth to be his people, his treasured possession* (Deuteronomy 7:1-6, emphasis added). *See 1 Peter 1:13-16; 2:9.

## The Church Is At War

Over and over the Hebrew Bible offers a physical picture of what the Church encounters spiritually. By studying the events that happened to the ancient Jewish people we can understand what we are contending with spiritually. God has an ultimate plan for the Jews in the coming years, and He has a purpose for each follower of Jesus right now! How do we receive the promises? We fight for them in the heavenlies!

*Finally, be strong in the Lord and in his mighty power. Put on the full armor of God so that you can take your stand against the devil's schemes. For our struggle is not against flesh and blood, but against the rulers, against the authorities, against the powers of this dark world and against the spiritual forces of evil in the heavenly realms. Therefore put on the full armor of God, so that when the day of evil comes, you may be able to stand your ground, and after you have done everything, to stand* (Ephesians 6:10-13).

The concepts of combat, conflict, and warfare have a repugnant ring to them. Because of this negative connotation Satan is able to render the Church ineffectual. Many believers miss God's divine purposes for them and, as a result, many more unconverted souls enter a Christless eternity. Yet the weapons with which we have been armed by God are spiritually mighty to demolish the strongholds of the enemy. But armor that is not taken up and put on is useless against the devil's schemes and attacks.

## Who Are the Children of God?

Why, then, if pews are full every Sunday with those professing that the Kingdom of God is here, does our society, even our families and personal lives, seem so unaffected? Can it be that numbers of those *considered* to be part of the Church are not? We have encountered many who show no evidence of the presence of the indwelling Holy Spirit. These could be the ones that Jesus must tell at the judgment throne, *"I never knew you"* (see Matthew 8:21-23).

The Gospel declares that when we enter into a covenant relationship with our heavenly Father through the shed blood of Jesus, He seals us with the Holy Spirit. Conversion as understood by the early Church was *"pouring **new wine** into **new wineskins.**"* The old wineskins were discarded. A distinct and noticeable change in the believing individual occurred. (See the Book of Acts.)

Today, the unconverted who call themselves "Christian" may in fact be those who have infiltrated our faith communities. The unconverted are owned by Satan to be used as he sees fit (see 2 Timothy 2:16). Infiltration is a most deadly enemy strategy. One of the difficulties we faced in Vietnam was trying to determine who was the enemy. They infiltrated our troops. On the outside they dressed and acted like everyone else even as they wreaked havoc in our midst.

***"So be on your guard! Remember that for three years I never stopped warning each of you night and day with tears"***

(Acts 20:31)

As part of our ten-year teaching retreat ministry Mike counseled church leaders. On one occasion a man (we'll call him Tom) came for some advice. He was battling sexual temptation as he counseled a woman who had recently begun attending his congregation. We talked for awhile and he left.

Several weeks later our family happened to attend worship at this church. At the end of the service there was a time of prayer ministry. The elders took up positions in the front. Because so many desired prayer that morning, they asked Mike to help. As he stood next to Tom, a woman came up for prayer. As she walked toward Mike the Holy Spirit impressed on him, "This is the woman Tom mentioned to you. She was sent here by Satan to seduce him. Pray for what she asks but do nothing more." When she walked away Mike turned to Tom and said, "That's the woman you mentioned to me a few weeks ago." Amazed, he asked, "How did you know?" Mike revealed what the Holy Spirit had told him regarding her satanic mission of seduction. Her cover blown, she was never seen at that church again.

On another occasion we were visiting a church and were surprised by the complete lack of male testimonies during a time of open sharing. On previous visits we had always observed a balance among the men and women as they spoke. Sitting there that morning Mike bowed and inquired of the Lord, "Why are there no men sharing?" The Spirit replied, "To your left are two women with a Jezebel spirit, sent here to inspire fear in the men to keep them from speaking." As Mike looked in that direction, he could see the two women whom the Spirit was indicating.

In prayer, he asked if there was anything he should do. The Spirit prompted, "You can pray to bind their influence here this morning." In the middle of prayer he glanced over to see both women glaring at him. At the end of the service he mentioned the situation to the church leaders. They recalled that the women had begun attending several weeks earlier, and that the testimonies of the men had dwindled from that point. The two women never returned there again.

In another congregation, the wife of one of the church leaders had trepidation about a woman who had been attending their church for about two years. This individual had become the head of the Sunday school program. One morning during worship the leader's wife recoiled in alarm at a demon that was perched on the suspect woman's shoulder. She insisted that the leadership look into the woman's situation. In their meeting the woman finally acknowledged that she had been sent by a satanist group to water down the curriculum of the Sunday school program. The lesson of this? Never lose sight that spiritual warfare is raging all around you, even in the most innocuous guises.

The following story was shared with group of church leaders who met at our retreat center from 1983-93. For years afterward, its intense truth would bring tears to us whenever we reread it. As you read, compare your own spiritual experience with that of the narrator.

## A Parable of War

(by Paul Knight, ca. 1986)

"We were sitting outside the village frustrated. We had been enlisted to defend and win the allegiance of the members of the village for the Crown. But there seemed to be so little response to the consistent goodness of the throne. We, the soldiers of the King, were growing tired and apathy was around us like a dense fog.

It was then that we heard the blast of the horns warning us that they were advancing. The Enemy, whom we had grown to hate and despise, was advancing his troops close to the village.

We knew full well that the enemy and his workers were ruthless. They breathed the fire of hatred. As the others around us began to speak, we knew that the village we were caring for and seeking to win would be devastated. One of the female soldiers with us began to cry out in alarm for the innocent children who would be devoured in the jaws of wickedness and deprivation. Her voice cracked with fear and urgency, for she had been one of their prisoners. Her scars, emotional and physical, were still fresh.

Those around the woman, knowing that the King had prepared us with a power far beyond that of our enemy's, stood in resolve to fight. We shouted to our fellow soldiers to stand and bear arms for the King, to defend the village and to fight against the advance of the army.

We sent messengers into the village, sounding warnings again and again that the enemy would take prisoners. We testified to the tactics of the enemy and to the promised care for those who follow the King. Some followed and took up arms with us. We resolved to defend to the end those left and to continue begging their enlistment under the King's banner.

When we returned to our camp outside the village, we again tried to rally our fellow soldiers to stand and to prepare for battle. The enemy had landed and was advancing with greater strength. We could hear the hellish cries of those who were being taken and those who so joyously performed the enemy's deeds of war. From the infants to the aged, we knew that they would be trampled and put in bondage. Untold horrors would be their fate. We again cried out to our fellow soldiers to stand and to fight.

A few of us ran to our fellow soldiers and with tear-filled eyes begged them to stand and to bear arms. But the fog had grown so thick, it seemed not only to block their vision but to silence our cries in their ears. They continued to rest and to talk.

One of our comrades was again explaining how to fight, how to use weapons. He was explaining the need to defend ourselves and the people of the village. With sweat on his brow and with great passion he began to lift our fellow soldiers up, urging them to stand. In panic he was running from person to person, propping them up, but they did not want to stand. In exhaustion, our comrade fell among them. We wept.

With greater determination we began to fight, still urging our fellow soldiers to stand. All around us the devastation, even of the King's army, began to overwhelm us. Still we cried out to stand and to bear arms for the One Who cared for us. We shouted out the names of the villagers. With fading breath we called out, "Help us, please fight with us. The enemy is here!"

In certain ways the Vietnam conflict parallels many of the spiritual warfare issues facing the Church today. Why were we involved in Vietnam? The lack of a clear reason divided this country. When Mike was in the Navy, his strategy and tactics classes emphasized the two "jugulars" of commerce in the world. Whoever dominated these two places could control the nations. The first vital artery was the Malaccan Straits near Singapore, through which a tremendous amount of world shipping passes. Second was the Straits of Hormuz between Saudi Arabia and Iran, over which vast quantities of oil are transported.

The US believed that it needed to keep the Malaccan Straits out of Communist hands; thus, our involvement in Southeast Asia. The USSR hoped to gain control of the Straits of Hormuz when it occupied Afghanistan. The Gulf War, too, was fought to dominate the Straits. Followers of Jesus need to fully understand the goals of our spiritual enemy, Satan. Misperception of his goals will divide us and keep us from fighting him effectively. The consequences are as eternal as heaven and hell!

The US participation in Vietnam began when Mike was in elementary school. He thought it would be over before he graduated from college in 1968. When we were dating, Sue sent for immigration information from Australia. They were recruiting teachers from the US, and paying substantial bonuses. We were really attracted to the opportunity before us. However, Mike was also aware of the tag, "draft dodger." His concern lay with his father, who enjoyed passing time with his friends at the Polish American Club each week. Since so many of these men had fought in previous wars, Mike feared they would misunderstand his reasons for teaching in Australia. Thus he went into the Navy, so that his dad would never be called the "father of a coward" by his friends. (Some people thought that concern for his dad's feelings was too shallow a reason to go into the military. That love for his father, however, resulted in three deployments to Vietnam.)

Not all followers of Jesus seem to have a global view of God's concern for all mankind. But if we follow Jesus, we cannot help but be burdened for those we know personally who may enter a Christless eternity. If our Father has sealed us with His Spirit, He will compel us to be burdened by what burdens Him.

How troubled are you about your unconverted family members, friends, schoolmates, co-workers? Is a demonic stupor keeping you from crying out consistently and fervently on their behalf? Then repent; renounce the spirit of stupor which blinds you and blunts your prayer. Ask your Father to burden you with the burden of His heart. His

Son's blood was shed to offer eternity with Him to those you know. If you have put loving trust in His Son, this has to matter to you!

One of Mike's closest friends fled to Canada rather than fight in Vietnam. He left the country out of deep conviction, not just to shirk military duty. Mike had, and still has, the greatest respect for him. Vietnam caused this nation to differentiate, as the Bible does, between those who act on their convictions and those who like to express their opinions.

Opinions mean nothing more than the air that comes out of one's mouth. Whatever you are spiritually convicted about will normally cost you something to obey. Conviction separates those who live abandoned to the will of the Father from those who are biblically knowledgeable but hold (and express) a lot of opinions (hot air).

## New Wineskins

God is looking for new wineskins filled with new wine. What do new wineskins look like to Him? *"If anyone would come after me, he must* ***deny himself*** *and* ***take up his cross*** *and* ***follow me****. For whoever wants to save his life will lose it, but whoever* ***loses his life*** *for me and for the gospel will save it. What good is it for a man to gain the whole world, yet forfeit his soul? Or what can a man give in exchange for his soul? If anyone is ashamed of me and my words in this adulterous and sinful generation, the Son of Man will be ashamed of him when he comes in his Father's glory with the holy angels"* (Mark 8:34-38, emphasis added).

The Lord is expressing the minimum standard for following Him. Our heart conviction combined with His powerful grace provides the means to fulfill His will. In this light, let us encourage and spur on one another to keep our wineskins pliable and useful for our Master's use.

May others discover in each of us what people beheld in the fishermen apostles when they were arrested: *"When they saw the courage of Peter and John and realized that they were unschooled, ordinary men, they were astonished and they took note that these men had been with Jesus"* (Acts 4:13). If we claim to follow Jesus, let's mirror Him in love, courage, humility, and forgiveness. Keep this firmly in mind:

**We are not always in the battle, but we are always at war.**

## Chapter 1

# The Anointing of the Holy Spirit: God's Power Given to Man

***"Christ the power of God and the wisdom of God"*** (1 Corinthians 1:24).

***"My message and my preaching were not with wise and persuasive words, but with a demonstration of the Spirit's power, so that your faith might not rest on men's wisdom, but on God's power"*** (1 Corinthians 2:4,5).

God's power is mightily underscored throughout the Bible.

The believers of the early Church understood the need for spiritual power if they were to penetrate their culture with the gospel. They were wholly dependent on the Holy Spirit to manifest that power in order for them to accomplish God's purposes. The authoritative power of Jesus's name propelled the Church into the conflicts it faced. Spiritual power in the name of Jesus was released through wholehearted trust in Him. That same trust and reliance on God's power are the vital elements needed throughout the Church today.

The restoration of the Hebraic heritage and relational priorities of the early Church is spreading throughout the world. At the same time, the restoration of the Holy Spirit's power is increasingly being manifested in the Church. As greater awareness of the vitality of spiritual gifts advances, followers of Christ are accessing a deeper recognition of their own individual gift(s). But knowledge of one's own gifts, although critically important, is incomplete, like a highly skilled basketball player with no team on which to play. The true testimony of the Lord's power at work in His people lies in the *cooperation* and *coordination* of the gifts His Spirit has bestowed on them.

> *We must pay more careful attention, therefore, to what we have heard, so that we do not drift away. For if the message spoken by angels was binding, and every violation and disobedience received its just punishment, how shall we escape if we ignore such a great salvation? This salvation, which was first announced by the Lord, was confirmed to us by*

*those who heard him. God also testified to it by signs, wonders and various miracles, and* ***gifts of the Holy Spirit*** *distributed according to* ***his will*** (Hebrews 2:1-4, emphasis added).

We must not drift away as our forefathers did. The reasoning and ecclesiastical dominance which they embraced still plague today's church. In God's sight, followers of Christ are connected to each other, for each one is a part of the body of Jesus:

*"Now about spiritual gifts* [or matters], *brothers, I do not want you to be ignorant....The body is a unit, though it is made up of many parts; and though all its parts are many, they form one body. So it is with Christ...Now you are the body of Christ, and each one of you is a part of it"* (1 Corinthians 12:1,12,27).

*"Instead, speaking the truth in love, we will in all things grow up into him who is the Head, that is, Christ. From him the whole body,* ***joined and held together*** *by every supporting ligament, grows and builds itself up in love, as* ***each part does its work****"* (Ephesians 4:16,17, emphasis added).

God's grace, *charis* (kair'-is), is activated in the heart of the individual who has a consummated relationship with Him through the Holy Spirit. Great power comes from the *synergy* of spiritual gifts (*charismata,* things of God's grace) as believers who are moved by His Spirit function together in harmony within the body to bring glory to the Lord. The manifestation of God's grace is seen in action, and He receives praise for those good works (see Matthew 5:14-16).

To help believers understand how spiritual gifts operate together, the apostle Paul uses an analogy of the human body. Reflect on the following verses as they pertain to our *individual* and *collective* obedience and service to Jesus. Note, too, the constant interplay of *one* and *many*:

*There are different kinds of gifts, but the same Spirit. There are different kinds of service, but the same Lord. There are different kinds of working, but the same God works all of them in* ***all men****. Now to*

***each one*** *the manifestation of the Spirit is given for the* ***common good****. To* ***one*** *there is given through the Spirit the message of wisdom, to* ***another*** *the message of knowledge by means of the same Spirit, to* ***another*** *faith by the same Spirit, to* ***another*** *gifts of healing by that one Spirit, to* ***another*** *miraculous powers, to* ***another*** *prophecy, to* ***another*** *distinguishing between spirits, to* ***another*** *speaking in different kinds of tongues, and to still* ***another*** *the interpretation of tongues.*

*All these are the work of one and the same Spirit, and he gives them to* ***each one****, just as he determines. The body is a* ***unit****, though it is made up of* ***many parts****; and though all its parts are* ***many****, they form* ***one body****. So it is with Christ. For we were all baptized by one Spirit into* ***one body****—whether Jews or Greeks, slave or free—and we were all given the one Spirit to drink.*

*Now the body is not made up of one part but of* ***many****. If the foot should say, 'Because I am not a hand, I do not belong to the body,' it would not for that reason cease to be part of the body. And if the ear should say, 'Because I am not an eye, I do not belong to the body,' it would not for that reason cease to be part of the body. If the whole body were an eye, where would the sense of hearing be? If the whole body were an ear, where would the sense of smell be?*

*But in fact* ***God has arranged*** *the parts in the body,* ***every one of them****, just as he wanted them to be. If they were all one part, where would the body be? As it is, there are* ***many parts****, but* ***one body****. The eye cannot say to the hand, 'I don't need you!' And the head cannot say to the feet, 'I don't need you!'*

*On the contrary, those parts of the body that seem to be weaker are indispensable, and the parts that we think are less honorable we treat with special honor. And the parts that are unpresentable are treated with special modesty, while our presentable parts need no special treatment. But* ***God has combined*** *the members of the body and has given greater honor to the parts that lacked it, so that there should be* ***no division*** *in the body, but that its parts should have* ***equal concern*** *for each other.*

*If* ***one part*** *suffers,* ***every part*** *suffers with it; if* ***one part*** *is honored,* ***every part*** *rejoices with it. Now you are the* ***body of Christ,*** *and* ***each one*** *of you is a part of it. And in the church* ***God***

***has appointed** first of all apostles, second prophets, third teachers, then workers of miracles, also those having gifts of healing, those able to help others, those with gifts of administration, and those speaking in different kinds of tongues. Are all apostles? Are all prophets? Are all teachers? Do all work miracles? Do all have gifts of healing? Do all speak in tongues? Do all interpret? But eagerly desire the greater gifts* (1 Corinthians 12:4-31, emphasis added).

> *Just as each of us has **one body** with **many members**, and these members do not all have the same function, so in Christ we who are **many** form **one body**, and **each member** belongs to **all the others**. We have different gifts, according to the grace given us. If a man's gift is prophesying, let him use it in proportion to his faith. If it is serving, let him serve; if it is teaching, let him teach; if it is encouraging, let him encourage; if it is contributing to the needs of others, let him give generously; if it is leadership, let him govern diligently; if it is showing mercy, let him do it cheerfully* (Romans 12: 4-8, emphasis added).

> ***Each one** should use whatever gift he has received to **serve others**, faithfully administering God's grace in its various forms. If anyone speaks, he should do it as one speaking the very words of God. If anyone serves, he should do it with the strength God provides, so that in all things God may be praised through Jesus Christ. To him be the glory and the power for ever and ever. Amen* (1 Peter 4:10,11, emphasis added).

The human body is made up of many separate parts, each with a distinct name and purpose. Yet the *association* of the body parts as they work in coordinated cooperation with each other makes the whole a fully functioning unit as the brain provides direction. As believers serve one another with their spiritual gifts in marriages, families, and intimate load-bearing relationships, the restored Church will be characterized by a visible cooperation empowered by the Holy Spirit. God's Word is true for all generations: *"'Not by* [human] *might nor by* [human] *power, but by my Spirit,' says the LORD Almighty"* (Zechariah 4:6). The *hope* that the Church so desperately needs will spring from the power of the Holy Spirit as He is manifested in and through God's people: *"May the God of hope fill you with all joy and peace as you trust in him, so that you may overflow with hope by the power of the Holy Spirit"* (Romans 15:13).

## The Language of Anointing

The spiritual anointing or empowerment noted in the Bible indicates a *holy setting apart* of a particular individual or thing by God unto Himself. Anointing signifies a call to a specific purpose or function to be accomplished on God's behalf. It is a sovereign act, akin in a sense to being drafted into the military. God chooses, anoints, empowers, directs; only He receives the glory. The person chosen for anointing is a vessel housing the Holy Spirit. Anointing equips a believer for a particular service to God through the Spirit's empowerment.

To set apart an individual, God may use a human intermediary such as Samuel, who anointed Saul (see 1 Samuel 10:1) and David (see 1 Samuel 16:13), or Paul, who anointed Timothy through the laying on of his hands (see 2 Timothy 1:6). Others were chosen directly by the Holy Spirit while they were yet in the womb, such as Jacob, Samson, Jeremiah, and John the Baptist.

A person anointed by God undergoes a process similar to what is experienced in learning a new language. Initially you begin to acquire a whole new vocabulary. You then learn syntax (word order), word accent, and sentence flow. When you are able to *think* in the new language without first having to translate it from your native tongue, you become fluent.

This process parallels growing in cooperation with the Holy Spirit. As you abide in Him, you grow in your understanding of the Spirit's voice and His direction for your life. Only through the Holy Spirit's anointing can you lovingly glorify your Lord. Your anointing is His means *to fulfill God's purposes* through you.

In any number of ways God can use your anointing within your faith community, neighborhood, or work place. *Each person* and *each faith community* needs to seek the Holy Spirit for *rhema* (specific application of the Word of God for a particular person or situation). Then you can be fully effective to *use* your gifts in *cooperation* with those in the Body who have other gifts.

As a follower of Christ, you need the Holy Spirit's guidance at three different levels:

- Knowledge of your own gifts.
- How your gifts can function with those of others.
- Which specific faith community of believers the Spirit wants you joined with.

One raindrop may not impact anyone, but the combined power of many drops can make a noticeable impression. One afternoon in Atlanta we were sitting in the glass-roofed lobby of a hotel. A fierce rainstorm broke out. As the individual drops smacked the roof, they rolled downward and joined with other drops to form successive waves of water. By the time the waves came to the edge of the roof, a veritable waterfall cascaded over the side walls to smash against the ground. So too the combined cooperative anointing of many believers can impact their neighborhood or their city for the Kingdom of Christ.

**Thoughts to consider:** Many of today's congregations place little emphasis on the Hebrew Scriptures, the Old Testament. As a result, many fail to understand the Holy Spirit's great importance. From beginning to end, the Bible makes plain that He is indispensable in every facet of our Christian life. The Spirit not only issues the call to fulfill God's purposes. He also empowers us to accomplish them.

The love, joy, and peace that we so desire are the fruit of the Holy Spirit working within us. We must no longer live as people who grieve or quench the Holy Spirit (see Ephesians 4:30). And let's be careful not to blaspheme the Holy Spirit by attributing His work to Satan, or by claiming that His giftings or purposes are no longer valid for the Church today.

## Hellenist Influence: Gift Interaction Is Lost

The New Testament reveals that the Lord Jesus trained His apostles for *ministry*. These men were the first to receive the indwelling Spirit: *"And with that* [Jesus] *breathed on them and said,*

*'Receive the Holy Spirit'"* (John 20:22). Through these apostolic agents God transmitted His revelation to His Church. It is evident from Paul's letters that God intended for spiritual gifts to operate throughout the Church age. Nowhere does Scripture indicate that followers of Jesus could ever do without the empowerment of the Spirit, the legacy of all who trust Jesus.

> *It was* ***he*** [Jesus] *who gave some to be apostles, some to be prophets, some to be evangelists, and some to be shepherds and teachers, to* ***prepare God's people*** *for works of service, so that the body of Christ may be built up until we* ***all reach unity*** *in the faith and in the knowledge of the Son of God and* ***become mature****, attaining to the whole measure of the fullness of Christ. Then we will no longer be infants, tossed back and forth by the waves, and blown here and there by every wind of teaching and by the cunning and craftiness of men in their deceitful scheming. Instead, speaking the truth in love, we will in all things* ***grow up into him*** *who is the Head, that is, Christ* (Ephesians 4:11-15, emphasis added).

Prior to the advent of the Church, the synagogues had been served by apostles, evangelists, elders, teachers, and deacons. After Pentecost, these synagogue functions became empowered by the Holy Spirit. When the apostles asked for deacons to be chosen to serve in the early Church, *"They chose Stephen, a man* ***full of faith and of the Holy Spirit****; also Philip, Procorus, Nicanor, Timon, Parmenas, and Nicolas from Antioch, a convert to Judaism"* (Acts 6:5; emphasis added).

The Greek, or Hellenist, philosophical approach that later so permeated the church and is widespread even today *theorized* about the meaning of the Greek words for these biblical roles. The more applicable and appropriate Hebraic approach encouraged believers to explore how these functions were understood and *lived out* in the synagogues and in their communities. The earliest followers of Jesus were Jewish. Because of their firsthand synagogue experience, they could determine the extent to which the Hebraic New Testament writers incorporated these practices into the Church.

The converted Greek philosophers who entered the church in the early centuries brought with them *syncretistic* practices, that is, heathen traditions and understandings that were alien to the Hebraic roots of the faith. As the Greek influence increasingly permeated the church, the original Hebraic understanding of *practical, everyday application* of God's truths waned. *Reliant dependency* on His grace diminished.

Pagan practices were accommodated and often adapted to more readily propagate the faith among the heathens. (If you have any doubts about this, consider the origin of the religious holidays that much of the church observes.) This readiness to adapt prepared the Church to assimilate the organizational system of the Roman Empire when Emperor Constantine issued the Edict of Milan in AD 313 to tolerate Christianity.

This Roman pattern of government established the ecclesiastical dominance and control that pervades much of the contemporary church. A man-made hierarchy of church power replaced the spiritual framework and purpose summarized in the preceding Ephesians 4 passage. A dramatic problem was created by this man-made system: the function of pastoring by *elders* changed into what has become known as "clergy."

This unbiblical mutation from elder leadership to clergy control continues to plague the church today. What a sad testimony of Church history. The Spirit's anointing has been quenched by systems of hierarchical control. Jesus told Nicodemus that the Holy Spirit was like the wind. Who can control the wind? Man uses its power, but can never control it. So, too, the Spirit empowers according to His will but is not captive to the bidding of men.

As you prayerfully go through this booklet, discern the pattern of mutual cooperation the Lord has ordained by giving spiritual gifts to His people. Note several points concerning gifts:

- A gift of the Spirit is a God-empowered *capacity for service* bestowed on every true believer without exception (see 1 Corinthians 12:7).

- These gifts are *spiritual empowerments,* not natural inclinations, so that the Lord can display His power through His people and receive glory and praise through them (see Hebrews 2:3,4).

- God bestows gifts as He wills so that they may be used for the *common good* of His people and for the *building up* of the Church: *"All these* [gifts] *are the work of one and the same Spirit, and he gives them to each one, just as he determines"* (1 Corinthians 12:11), and, *"So it is with you. Since you are eager to have spiritual gifts, try to excel in gifts that build up the church"* (1 Corinthians 14:12).

Spiritual gifts are given in power to be used in love. The love that God requires of His people as they function in their gifts can only be acquired through *humility*. As believers follow the prompting of the Spirit to use their gifts, they can better understand why 1 Corinthians 13, the "love chapter," is situated between two key teaching passages on gifts. The body must function *together* in accordance with God's plan so that all members may increase and be built up in love with Jesus preeminent in all things.

To love as Jesus would have His followers love requires that they humbly ask Him to expose and remove everything in them that is not like Him: *"In him you were also circumcised, in the putting off of the sinful nature, not with a circumcision done by the hands of men but with the circumcision done by Christ"* (Colossians 2:11). How we need grace to love as He loves!

Each believer should ask, "What gift has God been pleased to give me for service?" The gifts of the Spirit compel a believer to see the interdependence of the body of Christ. All of the gifts are important and necessary for the common good. No one should covet the gifts of others as did Simon the sorcerer (see Acts 8:18). As phrased by our friend Lars Wilhelmson,

- Every believer has some gift, therefore all should be encouraged.
- No one has all the gifts, therefore all should be humble.
- All gifts are for the one Body, therefore all should be harmonious.
- All gifts are from the Lord, therefore all should be content.

# Chapter 2
## Spiritual Gifts in Spiritual Warfare

The Bible portrays the Church in a state of war against the heavenly realms of darkness. Too often, however, the Church fails to see itself at war. Not only are God's children warned that they are engaged in warfare. They are also exhorted to fight with divine power:

*"Then the dragon* [earlier called Satan] *was enraged at the woman and went off to* ***make war*** *against the rest of her offspring—those who obey God's commandments and hold to the testimony of Jesus"* (Revelation 12:17, emphasis added).

*"He was given power to* ***make war*** *against the saints and to conquer them. And he was given authority over every tribe, people, language and nation"* (Revelation 13:7, emphasis added).

*"The reason the Son of God appeared was to destroy the devil's work...We know that we are children of God, and that the whole world is under the* ***control of the evil one****"* (1 John 3:8; 5:19, emphasis added).

> *Finally, be strong in the Lord and in his mighty power. Put on the full armor of God so that you can take your stand against the* ***devil's schemes****. For* ***our struggle*** *is not against flesh and blood, but against the rulers, against the authorities, against the powers of this dark world and against the* ***spiritual forces of evil*** *in the heavenly realms. Therefore put on the full armor of God, so that when the day of evil comes, you may be able to stand your ground, and after you have done everything, to stand... In addition to all this, take up the shield of faith, with which you can extinguish all the* ***flaming arrows of the evil one****. Take the helmet of salvation and the sword of the Spirit, which is the word of God. And pray in the Spirit on all occasions with all kinds of prayers and requests* (Ephesians 6:10-18, emphasis added).

> *For though we live in the world, we do not wage war as the world does. The* ***weapons we fight with*** *are not the weapons of the world. On the contrary, they have divine power to demolish strongholds. We demolish arguments and every pretension that sets itself up against the knowledge of God, and we take captive every thought to make it obedient to Christ* (2 Corinthians 10:3-5, emphasis added).

A warfare mentality demands that each soldier for Christ do his or her part through the power of the Holy Spirit. Much of the Church, however, has relegated the gifts of the Holy Spirit to something akin to an elective college course. Even in congregations that acknowledge spiritual gifts, the gifts are often viewed from a singular perspective, that is, helping an *individual* to discover his or her specific gift(s) for personal edification and information.

Whether at the level of home fellowship or congregation, the spiritual **coordination and cooperation** of the gifts to meet God's purposes for each faith community is rarely practiced. Two chief reasons underlie the paucity of coordination of gifts in faith communities:

- Failure to understand the nature of the spiritual warfare in which the church is engaged.
- Ignorance of the importance of spiritual gifts in contending victoriously in this struggle.

The Church was called to take the offensive in waging war against the powers of darkness. Satan has achieved a certain level of success by convincing many in the Church that there is no warfare. He has also deceived other believers into responding only defensively. Consider the words of Jesus in Matthew 16:18: *"And I tell you that you are Peter, and on this rock I will build my church, and the gates of Hades* ***will not overcome it****"* (emphasis added). Many believers have assumed a defensive posture against what they perceive as an attack by the gates of hell. Gates do not attack. A more accurate translation of that verse is, *"And I tell you that you are Peter, and on this rock I will build my church, and the gates of hell* ***will not withstand it****."*

Satan cannot withstand the coordinated assault of God's people. He has succeeded in keeping believers disorganized, but through the quickening of the Holy Spirit, that situation is coming to an end. Prophecies are being fulfilled as the Church is being awakened to the foundational truths that empowered the early Church. In conjunction with this restoration, spiritual gifts are being coordinated for offensive battle against the enemy so that the gospel may be more effectively preached.

One of the first assignments on which Jesus sent his disciples included preaching and expelling demons in His name: *"He appointed twelve—designating them apostles—that they might be with him and that he might send them out to preach and to have authority to drive out demons"* (Mark 3:14,15). Could this be the pattern of what Paul later refers to as the purpose for the Church: *"Now, through the church, the manifold wisdom of God should be made known to the rulers and authorities in the heavenly realms"* (see Ephesians 3:10)? Evangelist Ed Silvoso encourages the Church that through the shed blood of Jesus, we have authority in His name to give the demons "eviction notices." (See *"How to Reach Cities for Christ"* video series, from IBLP, Oak Brook, IL.)

It is imperative that we understand spiritual gifts in a *spiritual warfare* context. The significance of gifting is lost with a "peacetime mentality."

For instance, the gifts of prophecy, wisdom, and knowledge are more often manifested for "personal guidance" in many churches than for God's direction in fighting the battle. God has intended a specific purpose for each believer and for every faith community to do their part in the war. His people are to be discipled and trained to offensively engage the enemy through the authority of the name of Jesus: *"And these signs will accompany those who believe: In my name they will drive out demons"* (Mark 16:17), and, *"The seventy-two returned with joy and said, 'Lord, even the demons submit to us in your name'"* (Luke 10:17). Today, how many of the followers of Jesus can say, *"Lord, even the demons submit to us in your name"*?

The military mentality finds corroboration in Paul's references to Timothy, Paul, and Epaphroditus as soldiers. Soldiers are of necessity called to endure hardship, avoid distraction, and please their commanding officer (see 2 Timothy 2:3,4). Warfare requires *mobilization of troops, training,* and *coordination* in order for God's particular mission for each faith community to be fulfilled.

Consider the warfare ability and focus of your faith community in light of the following analogies:

- If you read in the paper that the US Navy was sending a ship on a 6-month deployment, the article would probably be of no interest to you unless you specifically knew someone on board. But what if you read that the ship was manned by 5,000 *untrained civilians* and that it was being sent into *battle*? As strange as this scenario may sound, many congregations operate in a like manner, ill-prepared for spiritual warfare. Believers do not have to hunt for enemy engagement. It is a given for all who belong to Jesus.

- Another analogy: You heard that all the military personnel sent to Operation Desert Storm had decided to take R&R, sunning themselves on the beaches of Saudi Arabia rather than carrying out their mission. Think of the consequences had they not followed their battle orders.

Neither the military nor the Church that Jesus Christ is restoring can exist in the manner connoted in these analogies. The Body, the army of Jesus Christ, has individual and corporate responsibility to its Commander-in-Chief.

***"Even a child is known by his actions"*** (Proverbs 20:11).

If you were driving by a military base and saw a whole company of soldiers leaving the base with cannons towed behind their trucks, you might conclude that it was an artillery company. If you observed a ship with a large flat deck covered with jets, you would suppose it was an aircraft carrier. If a large formation of fighter jets flew overhead, you might conclude that it was a fighter squadron. In the same way, you should be able to recognize the mission of each faith community by knowing the gifts the Holy Spirit has apportioned to it.

In light of this, consider two different, equally-sized congregations in the same city. Each group completes *Discerning Spiritual Gifts* in Chapter 5. The first congregation has a smattering of most of the gifts, but there is a heavy concentration, say over 40%, of helping, mercy, and hospitality. The second congregation has an equal representation of all the gifts with a concentration of evangelists and missionaries.

Beyond what the writer to the Hebrews calls the elementary teachings of the faith, the training and preparation for fulfillment of the specific purposes for each of these congregations will be different. The first congregation might zealously operate a soup kitchen for the local needy as a means of demonstrating the love of God. The second congregation might eagerly conduct effective evangelistic outreaches among ethnic groups within a city. Both faith communities long to reveal Jesus to the lost, but the activity of the Spirit in their midst has produced very different outworkings.

When you think of the different parts of the human body and the different units which make up the military, what parallels can you draw from the physical realm to help you understand the cooperation of the different gifts in your faith community? Not all people in the military are assigned to be "where the action is," that is, in combat roles. Most military personnel are in support roles such as logistics, medical, communications, maintenance. Although many of the people in these support roles have weapons training, fighting on the front lines is not their primary function.

The human body also contains action parts and support parts, each operating for the common good of the whole body. We are conscious of the action parts because they are visibly seen. But stop and think of the many internal organs of the body that enable it to operate. Unless there is some illness or disease affecting these parts, we seldom pay attention to them. Yet injury or illness to these organs with which we are seldom concerned is much more likely to cause death than would injury to an action part. You can function with a broken arm or missing leg, but not with a malfunctioning or missing liver, heart, or brain.

God has fit the organs of the body together in meaningful proximity to each other and has protected many of them within the skeletal framework. Would you expect to see an eye attached to the kidney or an ear to the heel? How about an artillery company attached to a medical battalion? Or twenty jet pilots stationed aboard a cramped submarine? The pilots would not only serve no purpose on board, their presence would also increase the discomfort level of all. Yet properly stationed aboard the submarine are a variety of skilled personnel whose combined abilities enable the submarine to fulfill its mission.

The specific assignments of all individuals and units in a war are designed for efficient and effective coordination to achieve victory. In the same way, the human body has been created for efficient coordination: *"But in fact God has arranged the parts in the body, every one of them, just as he wanted them to be"* (1 Corinthians 12:18). Have you ever pondered how to organize the body parts in a manner other than what God has designed? Isn't it wonderful that the elbow is *not* attached to the nose? The design of the human body permits it to function in accordance with the design and purposes of its Creator.

Within any military unit is a group of people whose training is directly linked to the mission of the unit. For instance, Mike was a pilot in a helicopter squadron during the Vietnam era. His mission was to fly combat supplies from cargo ships to replenish other ships with whatever they needed to keep fighting. His squadron represented one part of the logistical support for the combatant units. Also in his squadron (and equally important to the success of the mission) were administrative and supply personnel, and maintenance staff separated into divisions such as electronics, engine repair, and hydraulics.

Just as with the human body, each member of Mike's squadron was assigned a specific duty. The effective performance of that duty contributed to the squadron's overall ability to succeed in fulfilling its mission. This principle also holds true with the operation of spiritual gifts or with body parts. A "division of labor" exists so that the mission, goal, or objective may be met efficiently and effectively.

The establishment of deacons in the early Church was an enactment of division of labor: [Apostles speaking]: *"Brothers, choose seven men from among you who are known to be full of the Spirit and wisdom. We will turn this responsibility over to them and will give our attention to prayer and the ministry of the word"* (Acts 6:3,4).

Paul emphasizes a key point: It is not just a matter of a believer *having* gift(s). A wholehearted willingness for the Holy Spirit to *use* those gifts prompts each person to do his or her part. Paul encouraged his spiritual son Timothy, *"For this reason I remind you to **fan into flame** the gift of God, which is in you through the laying on of my hands"* (2 Timothy 1:6, emphasis added).

One congregation in the Midwest was loaded with mature believers who knew God was urging them to focus on neighborhood evangelism. Still, they were hesitant to begin. One key elder, in particular, feared failure.

We shared with this congregation that spiritual demonic powers can hold believers captive, fearful to obey God's prompting. (For more on demonic agitation, see our workbook *Demolishing Strongholds.*) A survey of the Body indicated that a majority were influenced by a spirit of fear and insecurity. By trusting in the authority of the Lord Jesus Christ, these believers renounced the work of the enemy and sought the Holy Spirit to fill them with power, love, and self-discipline (see 2 Timothy 1:7).

The first member to launch out into his neighborhood was that key elder. He admitted that he felt as though he were a jet on an aircraft carrier. He could see himself on the catapult ready to be launched but had held up all the other jets by his fear to go forth. Once his fear was cast down, he was able to hear clearly from the Holy Spirit and respond in His power. Then the other "neighborhood jets" followed suit in confidence to carry out their missions!

*Equal regard* for all the members of a unit is vital for the camaraderie needed to carry out the mission. Paul takes the same point of view when he discusses the differing body parts. When a military unit receives a commendation, all the personnel share equally in the recognition. David commanded equal regard from his fighting men: *"The share of the man who stayed with the supplies is to be the same as that of him who went down to the battle. **All will share alike**.' David made this a statute and ordinance for Israel from that day to this"* (1 Samuel 30:24,25, emphasis added).

**Authors' observation:** Sometimes believers operate from a prideful pit called "gift projection." They see their own gift as primary and feel that other believers should approach decisions from their particular outlook. Often because of self-focus, these individuals fail to recognize the importance of the perspective the Spirit is giving to others. Gift projection can be destructive to the overall ability of a faith community to fulfill God's purposes. When other gifts are demeaned or overlooked, the Spirit is quenched. We have seen this all too frequently in marriages and home fellowships in which dominant members hurt others through fleshly misuse of their gifting.

If our faith communities are to cooperate in the use of their gifts, we must also avoid the "sectarian pride" that Jesus experienced with His disciples: *"'Teacher,' said John, 'we saw a man driving out demons in your name and we told him to stop, because he was not one of us.' 'Do not stop him,' Jesus said. 'No one who does a miracle in my name can in the next moment say anything bad about me, for whoever is not against us is for us'"* (Mark 9:38-40). No single unit can win a war alone. If spiritual cooperation is to develop among home fellowships and congregations, pride and arrogance must be renounced.

## Three important prerequisites define a military unit.

1. The unit was created to perform a *specific mission*. The unit's mission is part of a broader objective being carried out by other units, each with differing mission assignments.

2. Someone in the unit has authority to lead it so that the mission can be accomplished. A military unit is normally led by individuals who are *operationally experienced* in the unit's primary mission, people who have previously participated in a similar type of encounter.

3. The *combined coordination* of trained personnel is required for the unit to complete its mission. All training and preparation are designed and coordinated to equip the unit to complete its specific assigned mission.

A person who enters the military is first sent to boot camp or officer candidate school (OCS), whichever is appropriate. There he or she is trained in general matters about military service. A key element of the training process is the breaking down of selfish ambitions, and instilling of awareness that he or she is part of a larger cooperative and mutually interdependent organization. (In a similar vein, the Hebraic early Church possessed what some refer to as "communal self-awareness." Just as the Jewish individuals were conscious of their personal identities as Jews, each also recognized his or her belonging to the Jewish family worldwide. In a similar manner, early believers recognized that each belonged to Jesus individually, yet each was also part of all believers everywhere.)

Following boot camp or officer candidate school, an individual attends further technical training. The soldier needs to learn the specific skill that will enhance the overall effectiveness of the operational unit to which he or she will ultimately be assigned.

During Mike's Navy career, when he completed OCS he entered flight school to learn the skill of flying helicopters. Upon completion of that training he was sent to a helicopter squadron to fly combat cargo missions off the coast of Vietnam. Likewise the soldier of Christ progresses from instruction in the rudiments of the faith to specific training in life application. He or she then identifies through gifting and confirmation the specific assignment in the faith community's mission.

## The Relational Progression of Our Forefathers

***individual ~ family ~ clan ~ tribe ~ nation***

To understand the relational coordination for spiritual warfare our faith communities need, study the pattern of leadership development and organization of ancient Israel when they went to war. Note the above progression. It moves from a *high relational—low organizational* mode on the left to an ever-increasing amount of organization as you progress to the right. The organization was derived from the relationships. An individual was related to his family. The family heads were related to the clan leaders. The clan leaders represented all the clans at the tribal level. All the tribes together comprised the nation of Israel.

- Elders who showed exceptional qualities of leadership as heads of families became clan leaders.
- Elders who showed exceptional qualities as heads of clans became tribal leaders.
- Elders who showed exceptional qualities as tribal leaders became leaders of the nation.

Mike and the other students in OCS were trained to be aware of the broader context of which they were a part. This is referred to as the operational chain-of-command. Each individual was required to know the name of his drill instructor, battalion commander, all the way to the current President of the United States. Each person aspired to move up the chain as leadership qualities were developed at each stage.

Let's look at a possible parallel for today's faith communities with the nation of Israel in the Hebrew Bible. The relationships within the Hebraic family were intimate. Such closeness decreased as one progressed through the clan, tribe, and nation. The tribe and nation levels required complex organization to function as fighting units, while the clan and family levels needed little organization.

| ISRAEL | FAITH COMMUNITIES |
|---|---|
| individual | individual |
| family | family * |
| clan | home fellowship |
| tribe | congregation |
| nation | congregations in a city |

The members of a family and neighborhood home fellowship enjoy great personal intimacy and require little organization. (* For the single, divorced, and widowed, the neighborhood home fellowship becomes an extended family, as it does for all who are load-bearers for each other.) Personal opportunity for intimacy decreases at the congregational level. Congregations and city-churches (all the congregations within a community) require greater organization to fulfill their cooperative missions.

Paralleling the development of leadership in the Jewish community the same progression occurred in the early Church.

- Elders who showed exceptional qualities in leading their families could become leaders of churches that met in homes.
- Elders who showed exceptional qualities in leading home churches could become congregation leaders.
- Elders who showed exceptional qualities in leading a congregation could become leaders throughout a city.

# Chapter 3
# Steps for Warfare Readiness

[Moses speaking:] *"So I took the leading men of your tribes, wise and respected men, and appointed them to have authority over you—as commanders of thousands, of hundreds, of fifties and of tens and as tribal officials"* (Deuteronomy 1:15).

## 1. Organized under Experienced Leadership

Wouldn't it be foolish if the men of Israel showed up for battle untrained, with no specific skills, no organization, no leadership? We know that this was not the case. When Israel's troops mustered for battle, they assembled as trained, organized fighting units commanded by men of experience in authority. We are told they showed up *"as one man"* (see Judges 20:11).

When God winnowed Gideon's army from 30,000 to 300, the warrior realized his need for an organized battle plan against the Midianites: *"Dividing the three hundred men into three companies, he placed trumpets and empty jars in the hands of all of them, with torches inside"* (Judges 7:16). Those in your faith community who have demonstrated wisdom and maturity can offer valuable insight for the direction of the congregation as you pray together. Those gifted with leadership can then implement the cooperative endeavors of the congregation in their mission.

In a war, distinct "theaters of operation" exist in which the enemy is to be engaged. Satan will attempt to diffuse your combined efforts through a myriad of activities for which you are not anointed. He doesn't mind if you spin your wheels in busyness, as long as you do not wage effective warfare against him.

Beware of the "loose cannons" in your congregation. These are the individuals who refuse to participate in conjunction with any other believers because they feel they know better or do not want the relational responsibility that true body life entails. Submission to one another as Paul calls for in Ephesians 5:21 augments the power and focus of the spiritual platoon as it penetrates territory formerly held by the enemy of our souls. It is the *coordinated* attack that brings down the gates of hell in the battle in which your faith community is engaged.

## 2. Trained for Battle

The Bible highlights a particular battle fought by Israel: *"Among all these soldiers there were seven hundred chosen men who were left-handed, each of whom could sling a stone at a hair and not miss"* (Judges 20:16). Isn't it correct to think that these men had been *trained* to use the sling in order to be so accurate? Who do you suppose trained them—men skilled with the sword or those who were proficient with a sling?

Consider another passage: *"These were the men who came to David at Ziklag, while he was banished from the presence of Saul son of Kish (they were among the warriors who helped him in battle; they were armed with bows and were able to shoot arrows or to sling stones right-handed or left-handed; they were kinsmen of Saul from the tribe of Benjamin):...Some Gadites defected to David at his stronghold in the desert. They were brave warriors, ready for battle and able to handle the shield and spear. Their faces were the faces of lions, and they were as swift as gazelles in the mountains"* (1 Chronicles 12:1,2,8).

These men were skilled in specific weapons and in the ability to fight well in mountainous terrain. Their skill and strategy were well known by Israel's enemies. The Bible tells us that a counter strategy was needed to lure the Israelites to flat ground: *"The officials of the king of Aram advised him, 'Their gods are gods of the hills. That is why they were too strong for us. But if we fight them on the plains, surely we will be stronger than they'"* (1 Kings 20:23).

*Mentoring* by those who have gained wisdom through years of experience in seeking and obeying the Lord is one of a congregation's most effective means to train and disciple soldiers for the Kingdom. Mentoring thrives on relational interaction from the heart of more mature believers with those newer in their faith walk. Coming together to prayerfully seek *rhema* for each one's assignment in the Body sets the stage for a lifelong practice of mutual availability and responsibility.

## 3. God's Guidance and Direction Are Critical (Never Do Battle Without Him!)

A key element of warfare, be it physical or spiritual, is precise guidance and direction in order to win the battle. An enemy will concentrate significant energy to disrupt lines of communication. His goal is to cut off a unit's ability to receive orders. He thereby reduces their effectiveness to efficiently coordinate their efforts.

It is imperative that God's people who are engaged in warfare operate under His direction. Isaiah issued a warning to those who seek the ways and counsel of men rather than God's Spirit: *"'Woe to the obstinate children,' declares the Lord, 'to those who carry out plans that are not mine, forming an alliance, but not by my Spirit, heaping sin upon sin; who go down to Egypt without consulting me; who look for help to Pharaoh's protection, to Egypt's shade for refuge'"* (Isaiah 30:1,2).

King David, a master of warfare, exclaimed of God: *"He trains my hands for battle"* (Psalm 18:34). David faithfully sought God's guidance before embarking on different military campaigns. God's directions for one battle were not always the same for the next:

*"Then David said to Abiathar the priest, the son of Ahimelech, 'Bring me the ephod.' Abiathar brought it to him, and David* ***inquired of the Lord****, 'Shall I pursue this raiding party? Will I overtake them?' 'Pursue them,' he answered. 'You will certainly overtake them and succeed in the rescue'"* (1 Samuel 30:7,8, emphasis added).

*"Now the Philistines had come and spread out in the Valley of Rephaim; so David* ***inquired of the Lord****, 'Shall I go and attack the Philistines? Will you hand them over to me?' The Lord answered him, 'Go, for I will surely hand the Philistines over to you'"* (2 Samuel 5:18,19, emphasis added).

*"Once more the Philistines came up and spread out in the Valley of Rephaim; so David* ***inquired of the Lord****, and he answered, 'Do not go straight up, but circle around behind them and attack them in front of the balsam trees. As soon as you hear the sound of marching in the tops of the*

*balsam trees, move quickly, because that will mean the Lord has gone out in front of you to strike the Philistine army'"* (2 Samuel 5:22-24, emphasis added).

David took the time to seek the *rhema* of God, that is, God's specific guidance and direct word for each battle. David even received from the Holy Spirit the plans by which Solomon was to build the temple: *"Then David gave his son Solomon the plans for the portico of the temple, its buildings, its storerooms, its upper parts, its inner rooms and the place of atonement. He gave him the plans of all that the Spirit had put in his mind for the courts of the temple of the Lord and all the surrounding rooms, for the treasuries of the temple of God and for the treasuries for the dedicated things"* (1 Chronicles 28:11,12). Everything that followers of Christ do on behalf of the Lord must emanate from the Spirit of God.

New Testament examples of God's guidance abound. Have you ever considered God's intervention through His angelic messengers? The Book of Revelation proclaims, *"The mystery of the seven stars that you saw in my right hand and of the seven golden lampstands is this: The seven stars are the angels* [messengers] *of the seven churches, and the seven lampstands are the seven churches"* (1:20). The letters to the seven churches begin, *"To the angel of the church of...,"* and conclude with, *"He who has ears, let him hear what the Spirit says to the churches."*

God is sending guidance and direction to His churches. Are His churches *looking* for His guidance, either through the Holy Spirit or through His angels? *"Are not all angels ministering spirits sent to serve those who will inherit salvation?"* (Hebrews 1:14).

The Gentile Cornelius received an angelic messenger, and salvation came to his household because Peter listened and obeyed: *"While Peter was still thinking about the vision, the Spirit said to him, 'Simon, three men are looking for you. So get up and go downstairs. Do not hesitate to go with them, for I have sent them'"* (Acts 10:19,20). God's guidance and direction are available to the Church for those who are seeking to hear. Inside your faith community, be it a home fellowship or congregation, how might God's specific will be revealed and confirmed today? Does He speak only to the authorities within your faith community? Or, does He also speak through apostles, prophets, and gifts of knowledge and wisdom?

Years ago while we were ministering at a retreat center, we visited a certain congregation from time to time. We knew the people quite well because of the numerous retreats in which they had participated. As we entered the sanctuary, the elders approached Mike, who has a prophetic gift. They told him, "God has indicated to us in prayer that He was going to speak through you for the direction we have been seeking from Him. Pray about this. Even if it takes months we will wait on the Lord."

As the worship began, Mike heard a prompting in his spirit: "Kneel down. I want to speak to you." For several minutes he received the future direction for the congregation to take. At the end of the service he reported this to the elders, whose spirits confirmed that the Lord had spoken to direct their path.

## 4. Holiness, The Essential Prerequisite for Victory

Jesus, the Head of His Church, is joining together every joint and ligament to fulfill corporate cooperation in His body.

The neighborhood home fellowship, built upon the Hebraic model of the early Church, is being restored as a place for God's people to be trained together to fight the spiritual forces of darkness. Encouraging and spurring on one another to uphold righteousness and to earnestly seek God's face will bring about much answered prayer: *"Therefore confess your sins to each other so that you may be healed.* ***The prayer of a righteous man is powerful and effective.*** *Elijah was a man just like us. He prayed earnestly that it would not rain, and it did not rain on the land for three and a half years"* (James 5:16,17; emphasis added).

A home fellowship of men and women mutually supportive in their gifting and trained by experienced believers can effectively fulfill the Lord's purposes. As an incredible fighting machine, they can "take the land" by bringing the message of life to the captives of sin.

God requires a righteousness of His people that leaves no room for compromise with evil. Our Jewish forefathers in the early Church understood the importance of repentance and confession in maintaining righteousness. They wanted their prayers answered!

> *The Lord your God will cut off before you the nations you are about to invade and dispossess. But when you have driven them out and settled in their land, and after they have been destroyed before you,* ***be careful not to be ensnared*** *by inquiring about their gods, saying, "How do these nations serve their gods? We will do the same." You must not worship the Lord your God* ***in their way****, because in worshiping their gods, they do all kinds of detestable things the Lord hates. They even burn their sons and daughters in the fire as sacrifices to their gods. See that you* ***do all I command you; do not add to it or take away from it*** (Deuteronomy 12:29-32, emphasis added).

The same emphasis — *no compromise with evil* — is declared to the Church:

> *Do not be yoked together with unbelievers. For what do* ***righteousness and wickedness*** *have in common? Or what fellowship can* ***light*** *have with* ***darkness****? What harmony is there between* ***Christ and Belial****? What does a* ***believer*** *have in common with an* ***unbeliever****? What agreement is there between the* ***temple of God*** *and* ***idols****? For we are the temple of the living God. As God has said: 'I will live with them and walk among them, and I will be their God, and they will be my people. Therefore* ***come out from them*** *and be* ***separate****, says the Lord. Touch no unclean thing, and I will receive you. I will be a Father to you, and you will be my sons and daughters, says the Lord Almighty'* (2 Corinthians 6:14-18, emphasis added).

*"You* ***adulterous*** *people, don't you know that* ***friendship*** *with the world is* ***hatred*** *toward God? Anyone who chooses to be a* ***friend of the world*** *becomes an* ***enemy of God****"* (James 4:4, emphasis added).

## Establish Your Perimeters of Holiness

A battle is fought by establishing perimeters, consolidating them, then expanding them. To be effective in spiritual warfare you must establish holy perimeters, beginning with your own home.

The Lord God chooses to dwell among His people: *"The virgin will be with child and will give birth to a son, and they will call him Immanuel"—which means, '**God with us**'"* (Matthew 1:23, emphasis added). The Lord is a holy God Who requires holiness among His people: *"Make every effort to live in peace with all men and to be holy; without holiness no one will see the Lord"* (Hebrews 12:14).

God regards friendship with the world as *spiritual adultery*, elevating the provocative system of the world to a priority level that surpasses God in importance to you. Believers are admonished to *"take captive every thought to make it obedient to Christ"* (2 Corinthians 10:5). Unrighteousness begins in your thought life; nip it there.

In order for God to dwell among His people in battle, consider the condition of holiness established in the Old Testament: *"As part of your equipment have something to dig with, and when you relieve yourself, dig a hole and cover up your excrement. For the Lord your God moves about in your camp to protect you and to deliver your enemies to you.* ***Your camp must be holy****, so that he will not see among you anything indecent and turn away from you"* (Deuteronomy 23:13,14, emphasis added).

Examine *your* dwelling place. Is there anything offensive to God that you *do* or *have* in your home? Believers with spiritual gifts of wisdom, knowledge, and discerning of spirits can help you to cleanse your home of unholy objects and activities. (To learn more about the importance of corporate holiness, see our book *Restoring the Early Church*.)

## Chapter 4

# Corporate Warfare Through Spiritual Gift Coordination

Spiritual warfare involves the eternal destiny of the souls of people. As you read the previous section, you may have become convicted or convinced that your gift(s) belong in a mutually interdependent alliance with those who have other gifts. The Holy Spirit Who apportioned to you His gift(s) will also guide you to the right combination of people so that you can effectively do your part.

To be successful in the spiritual warfare in which the Church is offensively engaged, followers of Christ must no longer view faith communities in the generic sense, *i.e.*, "a place to go to church," or "a personal sanctuary for worship and fellowship." We must discern the specific purpose(s) for those whom the Lord has brought together in community.

Each faith community should discover the gifts God has assigned. Frequently, just determining the gifts that are present can indicate why God has called the community to exist. Gifts of prophecy, wisdom, knowledge, and intercession can help believers receive the Lord's guidance and confirmation of the faith community's specific mission beyond worship and spiritual edification.

With a nod to technology, one congregation used a computer to tabulate the results of their spiritual gifts. The leadership had distributed a spiritual gifts survey to all the regular attendees. Based on the gifting that had been confirmed, members were agreeably placed in positions commensurate with their gifting.

The church leader who shared the results of this bold action commented to us, "I was amazed how many people who had been busy in the activities of the congregation were relieved when asked to step aside since their gifting had not matched their function. So many commented, 'I was only doing it because no one else was.' In the months since we reorganized based on spiritual gifting, our congregation has really begun to flourish. Everyone seems more edified." When God's people are permitted and encouraged to fulfill their anointing, they flourish as they serve in His power.

The majority of Paul's letters to congregations are written using the plural form of the pronoun "you." He is addressing each believer in context with his or her entire faith community. The "division of labor" that comes with the Spirit's distribution of gifts within our faith community enables believers to effectively wage war and to be interdependent with other faith communities.

Needing the gifts of others prompts followers of Christ to be less willing to take offense at anyone and more willing to live with an attitude of forgiveness. Interdependency also makes us more willing to be personally concerned when *"our brother sins."* Each of us needs the other to be in full fellowship with the Lord if we are to be effective in the battle.

The cooperative, God-given purpose of the gifts of apostle, prophet, evangelist, shepherd, and teacher is *"to prepare God's people for works of service, so that the body of Christ may be built up until we all reach unity in the faith and in the knowledge of the Son of God and become mature, attaining to the whole measure of the fullness of Christ"* (Ephesians 4:11,12).

Can you imagine the impossibility of ever fulfilling God's purposes or reaching unity together without the combined utilization of these gifts? If you were Satan and knew the purposes for which God has given spiritual gifts, how hard would you work to keep believers from co-operating together? What lies would you create to convince people that these gifts are no longer in operation?

Based on our experience with numerous congregations, we have grouped the spiritual gifts listed below according to function. (Note that this grouping is *not* the only way to view the gifts.) The organs of the human body do not function in precisely the same manner. A doctor must know both the purpose and the processes of each organ. For instance, the lungs and heart have two different purposes, and they also function in very different ways.

In order to effectively cooperate together, followers of Christ must take the time to understand the purpose and function of each person's gift(s). As you grow in this understanding and continue to walk in the Spirit, you will begin to see how dependent you are on the gifting of others within your faith community. Each person's *dependency* creates the *interdependency* of your faith community.

As you seek the Holy Spirit, He will guide you to the right place to be trained to implement your gift(s). To be effective, you must recognize and learn to appreciate the gifts of others with whom you are to cooperate.

- God speaks to *release His message* through gifts such as prophecy and tongues.

- God *reveals truths* through gifts such as apostle, teaching, knowledge, wisdom, evangelism, missions, exhortation, and interpretation of tongues.

- The Holy Spirit bestows gifts that produce *action to bless others*. These gifts include giving, healing, helping, mercy, and miracles.

- The gift of celibacy frees a person to be *specially devoted* to the Lord's purposes.

- The gifts of administration and leadership can see the combination of people and goals from God's vantage point and can give *recommendations and guidance* to achieve His purposes.

- The *calm certainty* that gives a believer a "reckless abandon" to the will of God is the gift of faith.

- The gift of shepherding is given to mature men whom the Father has bestowed *special nurture and compassion* for each person in His flock.

Understanding how the different gifts receive the Spirit's guidance and prompting is key to establishing cooperation in their use. Some believers are *spoken to,* others are *spoken through,* others are *prompted to act,* and still others are *prompted to tend the flock*. Each of the gifts plays a vital role, and each, like our own body parts, functions differently to fulfill its purpose. Some body parts function solely inside the body. The gifts of shepherding and administration may be viewed this way. Other body parts operate outside the body, such as arms and legs. These may be the evangelist and the missionary.

## The Cooperation of Spiritual Gifts in the Battle

Because of the programmed task-orientation of many faith communities, people may look for structural answers, for another program or for a by-the-numbers approach to incorporate spiritual gift cooperation into their congregation.

The authors were once interviewed to head up a new home fellowship ministry for a large congregation. During the interview we found that we could not communicate clearly with the interviewer. He was looking for programs and activities to occupy and coordinate the people as they met in contrived "care groups." In effect, he wanted a "Christian program" that would guide and instruct the small-group attendees so that there would be standardized, predictable outcomes.

A church leader from a large denomination once told us, "We can't have our people trusting Jesus as your writings call for. That would cause *mayhem*! We need to control and direct the actions of the people in our congregation." Do trust in God and obedience to Him *really* produce mayhem? *"For God is not a God of disorder but of peace"* (1 Corinthians 14:33).

As we have followed the growth of the Yoido Full Gospel Church in Korea, we are aware of a potential pitfall for believers who use this gifts booklet to prepare for spiritual warfare. God prospered the church in Korea through *wholly dedicated* human instruments who were *fully yielded* to the Lord's purposes. Yet many church leaders in this country discuss the growth of the Korean church in terms of human techniques and activity rather than of spiritual trust and empowerment. The Koreans see the Spirit of God at work; many American church growth experts see human factors such as those that have prospered the business world.

## One Skill, Many Applications...One Gift, Many Purposes

At the military base where Mike was stationed, there were several helicopter squadrons, each with a different mission. The mission of one squadron was anti-submarine warfare. Another performed search-and-rescue missions, and still another transported combat cargo. Each squadron was assigned helicopter pilots, but their respective missions differed significantly.

The specific function of each spiritual gift will vary in its outworking from body to body. In one congregation a group of believers with a mercy gift may operate a clothing bank for the poor as a means of meeting a need and building a gospel bridge. In another body, the mercy people may offer after-school care for the children of single working moms. There is great room for creativity within each faith community to encourage each member to serve in his or her gifting for God's glory. As your congregation works together to serve God, the unbelieving world will know that you are Jesus' disciples as you love one another (see John 12:35) and love them in His name.

If you belong to a very large congregation, do not be surprised if, under the same roof, there are *several congregations* with different yet mutually supporting purposes. The Holy Spirit will guide those who seek Him to combine people into effective units to fulfill God's various purposes. Seek Him!!!

If there was ever a purpose for the following passage of Scripture to be applied, it is to enable God's people to be where He wants them: *"Trust in the Lord with all your heart and lean not on your own understanding; in all your ways acknowledge him, and he will make your paths straight"* (Proverbs 3:5,6). If you let Jesus fulfill His own words, *"**I** will build my Church"* (see Matthew 16:18) as the Spirit empowers believers through His gifts, you will not have to prop up people with a myriad of programs. The neighborhood home fellowship that is based on the early Church model *is* being restored to both equip and train God's people. Within that intimate framework, believers can be coordinated to effectively wage war and bear spiritual fruit.

Take courage from these biblical reassurances of blessings to God's people:

> *"'For I know the plans I have for you,' declares the Lord, 'plans to prosper you and not to harm you, plans to give you hope and a future. Then you will call upon me and come and pray to me, and I will listen to you. You will seek me and find me when you seek me with all your heart'"* (Jeremiah 29:11-13).

*"And without faith it is impossible to please God, because anyone who comes to him must believe that he exists and that he rewards those who earnestly seek him"* (Hebrews 11:6).

*"And we pray this in order that you may live a life worthy of the Lord and may please him in every way: bearing fruit in every good work, growing in the knowledge of God, being strengthened with all power according to his glorious might so that you may have great endurance and patience, and joyfully giving thanks to the Father"* (Colossians 1:10-12).

Seeking God is crucial to receiving His blessing. Don't go on without wholehearted connection to the Source of life and His powerful working within you. Pray each day that the Holy Spirit will use you for the glory and praise of Jesus Christ!

# Chapter 5
# Discerning Your Spiritual Gift(s)

The best method to determine your spiritual gift or gifts is through the direct experience of prayerful, intimate participation with others in the Body. You need others from your faith community to be in meaningful contact with you throughout the week. Intimate relationships built on the load-bearing of one another's joys and burdens can help you confirm what gift(s) the Holy Spirit has apportioned to you.

This section was designed to help you discern your spiritual gifts through the help of *simulation*. The gifts that have been listed are only those *particularly apportioned* by the Holy Spirit, whether as manifestations or as equipping gifts. Any command issued to *all* believers, such as intercession or the practice of hospitality, has been excluded from this list.

- Beginning on the next page you will find the gifts listed alphabetically. Each gift contains a brief description followed by a list of statements that simulate different aspects of the gift.

- Read each statement. Using a scale from "0" to "10," place on the line next to the statement a number that describes the truth of that statement in your life today. Put a "0" if the answer to the statement is not current (*i.e.,* in the past three or four months). Place a higher number as appropriate for how you have seen the Holy Spirit **currently operating** in your life.

- Don't answer a statement based on aspirations of how you hope to someday serve God or how you may have served Him in years past. **Answer the statements based on your current actions and responses.**

- Total the number for each gift. List up to five gifts with the highest totals on the **Spiritual Gifts Summary** on page 53.

When you have completed all the pages and have ascertained your gift(s), **confirm your results** with others in your faith community. Confirmation by others who can attest to His gifting at work in you is indispensable. If the Holy Spirit is empowering you, Satan will do everything to keep you from that assurance. He knows that God will often guide your life based upon your gifting.

**Before you go any further, please pray for the Holy Spirit to reveal how He is empowering you at this point in your pilgrimage with Him.**

## Description of the Spiritual Gifts

(alphabetical listing)

You may find it helpful to the use the number guide below to complete the survey:

| | | | |
|---|---|---|---|
| never | 0 | moderately | 5 or 6 |
| seldom | 1 or 2 | often | 7 or 8 |
| sporadically | 3 or 4 | almost always | 9 or 10 |

### Administration

The spiritual ability to coordinate and complete the plans and decisions God has confirmed. (1 Cor. 12:28)

_____ I can delegate important responsibilities to others without having to oversee each detail.
_____ I am able to effectively organize people, resources, and time to reach a certain goal.
_____ I can focus on goals and develop strategies to reach them.
_____ My function in a group setting is to help people reach their goals.
_____ I follow through on details and make sure that whatever plans are undertaken are completed.
_____ **Total**

## Apostleship

The spiritual ability to be sent forth among God's people to build up and strengthen their resolve to trust and obey Jesus. (Eph. 4:11)

_____ I am not intimidated by cooperative endeavors with different faith communities.
_____ I have a call to work among all kinds of God's people.
_____ Other Christians are generally willing to follow the counsel I share with them.
_____ I feel called by God to be sent out by my faith community to begin a new work among those in need.
_____ I am recognized in several faith communities as a person with spiritual authority.
_____ **Total**

## Celibacy

The spiritual ability to remain contentedly single, resulting in more time and energy to serve God. (1 Cor. 7:7-9)

_____ As a single person, I am content in my intimacy with God and fellowship with others.
_____ I am uninterested in an intimate relationship with another person of the opposite sex.
_____ I am glad for the extra time I have as a single to better serve God and others.
_____ Sexual fulfillment has usually been low on my priority list.
_____ Being free from a committed relationship with a spouse has made me more available for the things God wants me to do.
_____ **Total**

## Discerning of Spirits

The spiritual ability to know with assurance whether what is said or done emanates from the Holy Spirit or from some other spirit. (1 Cor. 12:10)
_____ I can often perceive the particular spiritual gifting from which a Christian is operating.
_____ I am able to accurately judge between evil and good.

_____ I can distinguish which spiritual powers agitate or influence people.
_____ I recognize the work of the Holy Spirit in the events occurring around me.
_____ I can sense the presence of evil spirits in particular persons, places, circumstances, and objects.
_____ **Total**

## Evangelism

The spiritual ability to spread the gospel among unbelievers and to plant congregations, nurturing them to maturity. (See **Missionary** for cross-cultural evangelism.) (Eph. 4:11)

_____ I pursue friends and acquaintances who do not have a trusting faith in Jesus.
_____ I joyfully share with others why I serve the Lord.
_____ I eagerly discuss my faith on the job or wherever I gather with others.
_____ New faith communities have begun through my sharing and efforts.
_____ I am burdened for people to encounter Jesus and to grow in their relationship with Him.
_____ **Total**

## Exhortation

The spiritual ability to encourage, teach, and confront others to enable them to fulfill God's purposes through them. (Rom. 12:8,KJV)

_____ Those who are wavering or discouraged in their faith are strengthened when I share with them.
_____ I am able to spur on an apathetic believer to new heights.
_____ I enjoy challenging those whom God is calling to take a step of faith.
_____ I am able to strengthen and encourage those who feel defeated in their Christian walk.
_____ I can both empathize with and guide those who are in crisis.
_____ **Total**

## Faith

The spiritual ability to confidently confirm the will and purposes of God even if you don't fully understand all the details. (1 Cor. 12:9)

_____ I get excited when I face problems that only God can solve.
_____ I am enthusiastic about what I believe God will do in the future.
_____ I trust in the presence and the power of God to do the impossible.
_____ I can discern God's specific intentions for the direction of His work when others can't.
_____ I trust in the reliability of God even when circumstances appear hopeless.
_____ **Total**

## Giving

The spiritual ability to cheerfully and liberally contribute what is needed to benefit others. (Rom. 12:8)

_____ I am stirred to respond when I encounter those in financial crisis.
_____ I freely give to others in order for them to accomplish God's purposes.
_____ I feel a strong inner compulsion to meet the financial needs of others.
_____ If I earned more money, I could give more generously to finance God's work.
_____ I don't mind maintaining a lower standard of living in order to divert more funds for Kingdom work.
_____ **Total**

## Healing

The spiritual ability to serve as a vessel through whom God may heal. (1 Cor. 12:9)

_____ When healing is needed, I am stirred to pray for that person.
_____ The Lord often heals when I lay hands on someone and pray.

_____ I find great joy in bringing hope to those in need of healing.
_____ The Lord often uses me to bring physical and emotional healing to others.
_____ By learning more about God's ways, I can more effectively be used by Him to bring healing to others.
_____ **Total**

## Helping (Serving)

The spiritual ability to lighten the burdens of others by investing your energies and abilities on their behalf. (Rom. 12:7)

_____ I prefer to accept direction from others rather than give it.
_____ I am content to perform routine tasks that get the job done.
_____ I enjoy when others ask me to help.
_____ Last minute requests for help don't disturb me.
_____ I don't need public appreciation when I serve others, for my joy comes from serving.
_____ **Total**

## Interpretation of Tongues

The spiritual ability to translate and transmit a message spoken in an unknown language. (1 Cor. 12:10)

_____ I can interpret the message when someone speaks in tongues.
_____ I bring God's revelation to my faith community by interpreting what is shared in tongues.
_____ When someone begins to speak in tongues, I usually pray to interpret the message.
_____ When I interpret tongues, others are edified by what is shared.
_____ I feel an inner compulsion to help others understand a message spoken in tongues.
_____ **Total**

## Knowledge

The spiritual ability to communicate God's perspective for the well-being of others. (1 Cor. 12:8)

_____I study the Bible in depth to understand God and His will.
_____ I delight in exploring the different aspects of a faith walk.
_____ I enjoy discovering and sharing new insights of Christian truth.
_____ I want to convey God's truths so that hearers will apply them to their situation.
_____ I can discern and share deep understanding from the Bible.
_____ **Total**

## Leadership

The spiritual ability to motivate and direct others to accomplish the goals that God has revealed and confirmed. (Rom. 12:8)

_____ Strengthening and building up God's people is important to me.
_____ As the Lord directs my path, other believers follow my guidance with confidence.
_____ My leadership spurs on others to accomplish God's will.
_____ I am as concerned for the well-being of those who serve with me as I am for reaching God's goal for us.
_____ I motivate those who serve with me to use their gifts for God's purposes.
_____ **Total**

## Mercy

The spiritual ability to compassionately come alongside those who are suffering by God's will in order to meet their needs joyfully. (Rom. 12:8)

_____ I am prompted from within to make personal contact with the hurting and wounded.
_____ I am able to help the difficult-to-love without any expectation of gratitude.

_____ I encourage people in the midst of their suffering.
_____ I make myself available to comfort those who are distressed and hurting.
_____ I find joy in bringing comfort to the lonely and anxious.
_____ **Total**

## Miracles

The spiritual ability to serve as God's vessel through whom He performs supernatural acts. (1 Cor. 12:10)

_____ Because of the powerful working of God through me, people's lives have been changed supernaturally.
_____ God has used me to do miraculous things that provoke awe toward Him.
_____ God has intervened unexpectedly to do the impossible through me.
_____ I have been used by God to alter events and circumstances through a mighty display of His power.
_____ Things beyond human ability have occurred through God's use of me.
_____ **Total**

## Missions (Cross-cultural evangelism)

The spiritual ability to adapt readily to cultures and lifestyles other than your own for the sake of the gospel. (Eph. 4:11)

_____ My relationships with people of other cultures are very important to me.
_____ I enjoy learning other languages and/or customs so that I can better relate to people of different cultures.
_____ I identify easily with people from other races, languages, or cultures.
_____ I enjoy sharing the gospel with people whose cultural background is different from mine.
_____ I esteem the ethnic traditions and values of those from other cultures.
_____ **Total**

## Prophecy

The spiritual ability to receive and communicate specific revelations from God for His people at the appropriate time. (Rom. 12:6)

_____ I communicate important messages that I feel are from God.
_____ I discern and share what God is doing in particular situations in people's lives.
_____ God reveals messages and insights to my spirit to be shared with the Body.
_____ I speak boldly when I discern God's will in specific situations.
_____ I share messages of hope, strength, warning, or judgment.
_____ **Total**

## Shepherding (Pastoring)

The spiritual ability for the older men, the biblical elders, to father and nurture followers of Jesus to grow in spiritual depth. (Eph. 4:11, 1 Pet. 5:2)

_____ I am deeply committed to the long-term support of Christians as they grow in their walk.
_____ I go out of my way to bring spiritual nurture to the needy.
_____ Mentoring and strengthening believers bring me great satisfaction.
_____ Christians consistently look to me for encouragement and direction.
_____ I am able to spiritually motivate those who feel they can't trust God.
_____ **Total**

## Teaching

The spiritual ability to bring understanding and application of God's Word to others. (Rom. 12:7)

_____ I am able to help others better understand the basic principles of the Christian faith.
_____ I clarify passages in the Bible so that others will apply the truth to their lives.

_____ I delight in developing materials that encourage and deepen the faith of others.
_____ I am edified by opportunities to disciple believers into the way of spiritual obedience.
_____ I am able to share God's truths in such a way that believers are helped in their walk.
_____ **Total**

## Tongues

The spiritual ability to speak in an unknown language for personal worship, or for public edification if accompanied by interpretation. (1 Cor. 12:10)

_____ When I have publicly spoken in tongues, others have interpreted my message.
_____ I pray regularly in tongues as a prayer language to God.
_____ I am comfortable in settings where I can share in an unknown language.
_____ I expect that when I am prompted to share a message in tongues, it will be interpreted.
_____ Praying in tongues stirs my spirit profoundly.
_____ **Total**

## Wisdom

The spiritual ability to apply God's ways to life's situations. (Rom. 12:8)

_____ I am able to clarify the work of the Holy Spirit within those who seek my counsel.
_____ I can discern deep spiritual understanding that surpasses mere knowledge.
_____ I help believers understand God's will in decisions they must make.
_____ I can discern between my own human limitations and the particular insights that have come from God.
_____ When important decisions need to be made, I clearly sense God's guidance.
_____ **Total**

# Spiritual Gifts Summary

From the Totals line under each gift, list on the lines below the gift(s) that you consider significant in your life. There may be just one or several. Does your spirit feel right about what you have listed below? Ask others who are close to you spiritually to review these gifts and to confirm their accuracy.

1. __________________________

2. __________________________

3. __________________________

4. __________________________

5. __________________________

Based upon the gift(s) the Holy Spirit has apportioned to you, God will use you to further His purposes. At the same time, Satan will attack you in these areas to keep you ineffective as you seek to fulfill God's objectives. A frequent tactic is distraction through a myriad of church-related activities, none of which God has called you to.

Seek confirmation from those who know you well and are mature in the Lord. Your ongoing intimacy with the Lord is vital if you are to be about His affairs in His power and timing. Pray to discern how God wants to use you in your congregation as well as in your neighborhood and workplace.

# Chapter 6
# Development and Use of the Gifts

Over the years we have observed the use of spiritual gifts among a wide variety of faith communities. Very beneficial to all believers who are seeking full effectiveness in the Body has been access to mature believers who are operating faithfully in the Spirit's gifting. Mentoring is a biblical means of modeling godly participation in the Body. Note Paul's counsel regarding pressing on to the goal: *"Join with others in following my example, brothers, and take note of those who live according to the pattern we gave you"* (Philippians 3:17).

God is very creative in His use of those who are fully yielded to His purposes. Your exposure to the variety of ways in which He operates through the empowerment in gifts enhances and strengthens your cooperation with Him and with one another. The notes below are intended as encouragement and caution. They are certainly not restrictive for every person or situation.

## Administration

Through the gift of administration the Holy Spirit brings understanding of the methods and resources needed to complete God's purposes. Administrators need to know the gifting of others in the Body so that they can help each believer discover how to cooperate with others to fully walk as a functioning spiritual family in the Lord. Mentoring by those who are experienced in administration will help you see the value and needs of those with other gifts. Beware of a focus on task completion that fails to consider the feelings and gifting of the people who are needed to complete the task. Overemphasis on tasks may lead to control and manipulation, bringing apprehension to others in the Body.

Because of their insight and awareness into the different elements of the mission, those gifted with administration may grow frustrated if the objective is not readily achieved. Regrettably, many clergy find themselves trying to fill this role without the Spirit's anointing, and are suffering burnout as they plod ahead ineffectively.

## Apostleship

Underlying the gift of apostleship is an attitude of servanthood that only Christ can bring about. Since apostles are sent forth to accomplish a specific purpose among different faith communities, they need the refining fire of the Spirit to develop compassion for those who are struggling in their walk. Often believers gifted with apostleship have operated in other giftings over the years, and have become discerning of the motives of others. As faith communities continue to grow in cooperation with one another, this gift will grow in importance because of the genuine servant leadership these believers will exhibit as they carry truths from place to place.

## Celibacy

Both Jesus and Paul refer to those who have a special gifting that enables them to fulfill their life purposes without a life partner. Unfortunately, all too often those in congregations fail to include single believers as true family members. Thus, singles may feel reproach or unspoken disdain from other believers because they don't fit into society's pattern. To forestall the loneliness with which Satan attacks them, these individuals need an extended family, a home fellowship, for support and load-bearing. If you have this gift, you have been presented the wonderful privilege to serve God wholeheartedly without encumbrances and to re-focus other believers on the sufficiency of God to fulfill every life need.

## Discerning of spirits

This gift functions as a spiritual early-warning device to discern whether something is of God or of Satan. Regrettably, in many faith communities the deceiver has convinced believers that spirits don't exist or that discernment is irrelevant. In several congregations worship leaders have admitted that they are at times tempted to "conjure" a mood for worship, much like the priests of Baal tried to conjure their god when confronted by Elijah. God will not be conjured by mood. He is approached by those with clean hands and a pure heart who need no mood enhancement. Those gifted with discerning of spirits can sense a conjuring motivation even when the rest of the faith community is oblivious. This gift should be incorporated into

Body life by testing spirits for truth or lies (see 1 John 4:1), discerning unrighteousness within people's homes, and assisting in congregational decision making. To operate without discerning of spirits leaves God's people open to ruses by the devil, such as the Israelites experienced with the Gibeonites (see Joshua 9).

**Author's Note:** As Mike was writing about *conjuring* during worship, Sue handed him David Wilkerson's 7-29-96 newsletter. Wilkerson had been visiting other congregations and he wrote,

> It turned out to be a heartbreaking experience for me. Over the past few years, our ministry has received thousands of letters from across the nation from spiritually starved Christians who have told us they can't find a church that meets their deepest needs. I used to think, 'Could that be possible? Are there that many dead, shallow churches in this country? Perhaps those writing to us are too critical.' But after what I saw and experienced that Sunday morning, I now know they are right. The worship leader used every possible gimmick to pump up the crowd. He told jokes, jumped around, pleaded and scolded the congregation. The result was hyped-up noise, too distracting to allow for genuine worship and praise.

### Evangelism

Like his counterpart in the synagogue, the evangelist in the early Church was a church planter and repairer in the pattern of Paul, Timothy, and Titus. *He established local bodies and assisted churches through tough times.* The evangelist exercised spiritual authority to anoint the older, spiritually mature men who were qualified to be elders. When the hierarchical structures of the Roman Empire entered the Church, this gift was relegated to history.

Many churches have misapplied Jesus' words in Matthew 28:18-20 (the "Great Commission") to pressure all believers to be evangelists. Although followers of Christ should share their faith and make disciples in the normal course of living for Jesus, that does not make one an evangelist. The growth of the early Church happened through fellowship in homes: *"Every day they continued to meet together in the tem-*

*ple courts. They broke bread in their homes and ate together with glad and sincere hearts, praising God and enjoying the favor of all the people. And the Lord added to their number daily those who were being saved"* (Acts 2:46,47).

A number of contemporary evangelists, who are actually church planters, are often inappropriately placed in the position of "pastor." Some have started faith communities only to eventually destroy them by failing to appoint and anoint biblical elders to pastor the community. As the faith community initially grows, inordinate expectations for nurture and teaching may be placed on the evangelist who is not gifted in these areas. If the fatherly functions of caring for the flock's needs are not met by the elders, people will leave to find relationships where they can be nurtured in Christ.

## Exhortation

A mature gift of exhortation provides the best combination of wise encouragement on one hand and admonition on the other. In many faith communities, however, admonishment is no longer acceptable, even though the Bible calls for it. Exhorters have for the most part been jumping on one foot, *i.e.,* encouraging without exercising reproof when it is needed. Believers with this gift need prayer and emotional support from others in the Body to fulfill their total contribution to their faith community. The world system continues to encroach upon the Church; exhorters are instruments in God's hands to encourage righteousness.

## Faith

The spiritual gift of faith is seldom understood. Our cognitive, rational church culture has to know all the "pros and cons" about a matter before it can decide what God's will is. Believers with the gift of faith know and trust God without having to understand how He will accomplish His promises. These believers seem to get more excited as circumstances become more desperate. They are sure from deep within their spirit that God will show Himself strong. Those with Spirit-empowered faith can encourage and strengthen others to trust God to reveal His will and to empower His people to fulfill it.

## Giving

The marvelous, selfless gift of giving may be frustrating to those who don't have it, particularly to spouses and family members. Givers are often motivated to sacrifice beyond their means, which can frighten or irritate other family members. In faith communities, believers motivated by giving tend to rattle budget meetings with what appears to be living on the edge, eager to distribute God's whole storehouse. Givers can refresh the hearts of many by their joyful generosity and are sorely needed throughout our faith communities. He Who owns the cattle on a thousand hills is more than able to provide the means for unabashed, Spirit-directed giving in the Body.

## Healing

Many believers who have gifts of healing are hesitant to walk in them. They are concerned about sensationalism or fearful that the person for whom they pray might not be healed. Satan does not want the Lord glorified through visible healing. He therefore influences those in the congregation to acclaim the person with healing gifts rather than attribute the glory to God. The believer with this gift is merely an intermediary for God's grace to heal. He or she needs protection and accountability within his or her faith community to avoid the schemes of the enemy.

## Helping (Serving)

God visits many people through the enactment of this gift, yet He often goes unnoticed and receives no glory. Often the gift is viewed as human volition rather than spiritual empowerment. Those who are blessed by the helper's efforts heap praise and appreciation on the individual who is serving rather than on God Who has bestowed the gift. The gift of helping, along with mercy, illustrates the tender heart of God. Believers who are gifted with helping should be especially conscious of the temptation to seek recognition for a job well done, and be content with joyful service *"as unto the Lord."*

## Interpretation of tongues

The Holy Spirit speaks as He wills through a believer with this gift in order to build up the Body. When a tongue is spoken in public it must be interpreted or the speaker should sit quietly. The public use of the gift of tongues is the Holy Spirit's means of edifying the faith community through interpretation. Mike was in a worship service once when an emotional prayer was offered up in a language he didn't understand. In response to his prayer to grasp the meaning, the Spirit moved on him to share in English what had been spoken. After the service, those who understood the woman's language remarked that his interpretation had been accurate and encouraging. (See the gift of tongues, below.)

## Knowledge

If you have the gift of knowledge, beware of pride, particularly if you are a new believer. The enlightenment and understanding revealed by the Spirit may cause you to think more highly of yourself than you ought (see Romans 12:3). Such self-exaltation may lead you into fleshly knowledge rather than Spirit-guided understanding. Discipleship in the Word and intimacy with the Father will attune you to discernment that the words you share are indeed from the Spirit of Truth.

## Leadership

Mentoring and proven obedience to the Holy Spirit are necessary prerequisites for this gift to be effective. Many in leadership roles may be operating from natural inclination or fleshly motivation rather than from spiritual gifting. Because of current practices in choosing leaders, a number of faith communities select individuals who *control* and *direct* the affairs of people. These leaders do not lead as the Bible calls for — they *command*. The leadership that is gifted by the Holy Spirit is upright in character and epitomizes a *servanthood lifestyle* for others to follow. Believers with this gift are strongly influenced by their responsibility to God and are diligent to uphold His purposes within the community they are serving.

## Mercy

Because the gift of mercy carries with it the tender compassion of the heavenly Father, Satan has designed special traps for those with this gift. Some who claim to have the gift of mercy are in reality controlled by a fear of rejection. Their kind actions are actually attempts to forestall rejection.

When God is in the process of chastising and disciplining someone for sin, a person gifted with mercy may get involved at the wrong time. God may be bringing to repentance the one He is disciplining, and an inappropriate use of empathy may prolong the discipline process. Those with the gift of mercy should seek confirmation from others in their faith community before they step in.

Satan may influence a mercy person to listen to slander and gossip, especially over the telephone. Satan counts on that person's compassion to listen to stories of woe that often contain bitter resentment that defames a third party. As a result, one-sided, derogatory slander about another person is shared. This results in tension that affects the mercy person's life and relationships. Repentance for entertaining slander is a must if he or she is to truly represent God in Spirit-led mercy.

## Miracles

God is still working miracles through His people. A believer with the gift of miracles faces the same danger of personal notoriety and pride as does the individual with gifts of healing. Satan is only too eager to pervert the action and motivations of someone with this gift. Other members of the Body can serve as a safeguard of discernment and accountability in order that God alone receives the glory for His work.

## Missions (Cross-cultural evangelist)

A missionary is a cross-cultural evangelist who fulfills the church planting role. (See Evangelism, above.) Believers with this gift have an eagerness to relate to people of other cultures, and to develop friendship bridges that will prepare the way for effective gospel sharing. Those with this gift who remain in their native land are often creative in their means of accessing internationals. Some initiate English language classes, cooking classes, crafts sessions, or car repair lessons. Many believers with the gift of missions have a relatively low regard for their own material needs and require input and participation by other Body members to ensure that family needs are being met adequately.

## Prophecy

The gift of prophecy requires order and must be under the control of the prophet. Prophets in particular benefit from mentoring (see 1 Corinthians 14:32), as God may bring a message to a person with the gift of prophecy, but the timing for delivery may not be immediate. Many who are untrained in prophecy open their mouths too quickly. God has precise timing for the delivery of His message.

We discovered in the late 1980's that many individuals with the gift of prophecy had been driven from their faith communities. Some had delivered their message with attitudes of condemnation or arrogance. Others had allowed unrighteousness to enter their lives. Still others had shared messages regarding God's displeasure with tolerated sin and had incited the leadership's wrath. Messages brought forth from believers with this gift should be subjected to testing to verify that the origin is of God (see 1 John 4:1).

## Shepherding (Pastoring)

This gift, which was modeled by the elders in the synagogue and at the city gates, has become an occupation within the Church rather than Spirit-empowered nurturing by wise and mature elders. Through the influence of the Greeks and Romans, God's Word was violated as titles were bestowed, elevating it to something the Spirit never intended.

A healthy congregation will have several elders who are empowered by the Spirit to nurture and train other believers into maturity. The full purpose of pastoring is seen when it is used in conjunction with other gifts so that each disciple in the Body can bear much fruit.

## Teaching

The spiritual gift of teaching in the early Church was not the oratorical lecture style often practiced in our faith communities today. That method was acquired from the Greek philosophers. The gift of teaching emanates from knowing God and applying His Word. It addresses God's truth to particular situations so that His people may establish *halakhahs* in their lives. *Halakhah* is a Hebrew word for the *way* the Word of God is applied to particular life circumstances. The elders of the early Church, the biblical gray-haired *zakens*, were required to be able to teach, that is, to apply the Word of God to the state of affairs of those they were mentoring. Thus the hearer was equipped to become a *doer* who could more obediently walk in conformity with Jesus.

## Tongues

The gift of tongues is bestowed for the purpose of personal edification with the Lord (see 1 Corinthians 14:4) and for edification of the whole faith community when the message is interpreted. Some congregations have encountered those who have spoken in tongues publicly but have not brought forth *"some revelation or knowledge or prophecy or word of instruction"* (see 1 Corinthians 14:6) that can then be interpreted. This situation is unfortunate, as edification of the Body comes only with the understanding brought by interpretation. Use of the gift of tongues in public should never become distracting for other worshipers or spotlight attention on the individual.

## Wisdom

Wisdom is highly prized and sought after all throughout Scripture. God's people are repeatedly urged to acquire wisdom. People anointed with the gift of wisdom apply God's practical advice and counsel to the life situations of others. Human wisdom requires a combination of knowledge and experience. Spirit-empowered wisdom, however, comes through divine inspiration. At times even the one who is sharing the gift of wisdom is surprised by what is spoken!

# Chapter 7

# Reflections for You and Your Faith Community

1. Through the influence of Hellenist (Greek) philosophers, the western church has lost the relational progression that strengthened the early Hebraic Church. As the Hebraic influence disappeared, religious practice centered around impersonal meetings in structures that were modeled after pagan temples. As these worship buildings proliferated, the interpersonal strength and power of the earliest believers were lost.

   The restoration of neighborhood home fellowships based upon the early Church model can return a balanced view of the importance of all the spiritual gifts. The past fifty years have witnessed a restoration of the "equipping gifts," *i.e.*, apostles, prophets, evangelists, shepherds, and teachers, to prepare God's people to *fulfill His purposes*. The full unity of the Church will enable it to fight for the spiritual control of our cities. This will be accomplished only when the cooperative empowerment of the equipping gifts is once again demonstrated within and among our home gatherings and congregations.

2. A building is not a church, nor can it ever be. Only people who have placed their trust in Jesus can be called the "church," the "called-out ones." Rethink what you call the building in which you gather for worship. Wherever God's people are during the week is where His Church is. Ask yourself:

- What are you doing through God and for His glory each day?
- How are your efforts being coordinated and supported by your faith community?
- How are the people of your faith community being trained?
- What practical experience do those who are training others have?
- What mission has God assigned to your faith community?

3. Much of the western church has connoted "one building equals one congregation." In reality, when spiritual gifts are discovered and organized into meaningful groups and the missions of each group have been revealed by God, several congregations may meet in one location. Congregations that are relationally trained and organized through the gifts of the Spirit can be coordinated to operate like a fleet of ships. A fleet may comprise submarines, guided missile cruisers, aircraft carriers, and so on. All the ships are coordinated in order to cooperate with the others to fulfill the common mission of the whole fleet.

   Within each ship there are different unique departments that cooperate together to fulfill the specific capabilities of the ship. Many responsibilities that are not directly related to the ship's mission still must be carried out for the ship to function: food preparation, laundry, supply administration, duty scheduling. Yet it is the *totality* of the ship's personnel working together that enables the mission to be accomplished.

   Ponder this scenario for a moment. A particular group of elders filled with primary gifts of mercy and helping are serving in a congregation whose primary gifts are also mercy and helping. Could it be that the Holy Spirit has chosen these men to train the people to fulfill a mission of mercy and helping? This is exactly how the spiritual warfare of the Church is to be carried out: experienced leaders depending on the anointing of the Holy Spirit and applying their previous experience as they train believers to carry out the mission.

   Consider another hypothetical situation. Suppose two of the four elders in a faith community have the gift of evangelism and two have gifts of mercy and administration. Can you see a possible tension as they serve their congregation? Is it possible that there may be two mutually supportive congregations within this one Body of believers, each with its own specific mission, and relationally coordinated by the leadership?

   All of the gifts are necessary for each congregation to function as a body, yet a preponderance of a particular gift could indicate a specific mission from God for that faith community. Your ultimate goal is to share the gospel and make disciples, but unbelievers often need a bridge of contact before they have "ears to hear." How can *your* faith community reach the unsaved through the cooperation of spiritual gifts within it?

*The elders need to discern the gifts the Lord has apportioned to their faith community.* They must prayerfully identify their focus and mission in order to ensure that each member with his or her unique gifting is trained to participate. To expect one individual to train all the members to fully walk in their diverse giftings would be unfeasible and unsupported by Scripture. Paul instructs Timothy to entrust the truth to *"reliable men who will also be qualified to teach others"* (see 2 Timothy 2:2).

In each congregation there are probably mature believers capable of training up newer Christians in effective use of their gifts for the common good. The prophets in the Old Testament had their gifting and ministry developed by other more experienced prophets: *"The* ***company of the prophets*** *at Bethel came out to Elisha and asked, 'Do you know that the Lord is going to take your master from you today?'* (2 Kings 2:3, emphasis added). (See also 2 Kings 6:1; 9:1.) Who better to train a prophet than an experienced prophet? Might this be true regarding other gifts?

4. The goal of victory in a war or even in a battle must be broken down into smaller, manageable, achievable tasks. To identify the elements that can lead to spiritual victory, think about how the gifts of administration, prophecy, wisdom, and knowledge can contribute to the effectiveness of winning the fight against Satan and to facilitate the spread of the gospel. Can you readily identify in your faith community the believers with those particular gifts?

5. A key question in a war is, "What are we fighting for?" In spiritual warfare, Christians are seeking God's power and authority to battle Satan for the souls he is holding captive. These prisoners are the individuals we know, our neighborhoods, our cities, and the regions beyond. We need to regard the lost as captives imprisoned behind the gates of deceit and delusion that Satan induces in people.

A primary Church objective is to free people from spiritual captivity in the name and power of Jesus Christ so that they might have a life-giving relationship with Him. For the sake of individuals and neighborhoods, believers must wage war through the coordinated warfare prayer of neighborhood home fellowships. Through the combined effort of congregations, we can prayerfully fight on behalf of our cities.

6. The cooperation of congregations throughout a city will be increased by the Lord as the influence of the Greek philosophical spirit loses its control in the western church. Philosophically constructed "doctrines" that now divide the church into non-cooperative and opposing camps are being judged for the fruit of division and strife that they have produced. The Greek influence has caused believers to divide cities by denominational representation, with little or no cooperation in fighting together to take and to hold our cities for Jesus. Through gangs, violence, immorality, and drugs, Satan has effectively taken over our cities. The *Church*, not the police, needs to take the spiritual offensive at this time.

   Would Paul be able to greet the churches in your city today with the same expectation of full cooperation that he anticipated in Galatia and Colosse? *"And all the brothers with me, To the **churches in Galatia**"* (Galatians 1:2), or, *"After this letter has been read to you, see that it is also read in the **church of the Laodiceans** and that you in turn read the **letter from Laodicea**"* (Colossians 4:16, emphasis added).

   As the Lord undoes the influence of the Greek spirit that now divides our churches, we believe that the cooperative attitude demonstrated among the early churches to which Paul wrote will be restored. How wonderful will be the time when we can speak about the "church at Colorado Springs" and the "church at New York City"!

7. People influence each other's behavior. Paul tells us that even some in the church community are influenced by Satan for his purposes: *"And that they will come to their senses and escape from the trap of the devil, who has taken them captive to do his will"* (2

Timothy 2:26). Many people within the church live like POW's. They subsist on the crumbs of religious practices tossed them by their demonic captors who hold them through oppression and fear. Many of these captives do not realize how Satan is manipulating them. Often they are used to discourage others in their faith communities by hindering their confidence to fully trust in Jesus.

Note in the following passage the importance of interpersonal influence as it may affect believers in your faith community:

> *When you are about to go into battle, the priest shall come forward and address the army...He shall say: 'Hear, O Israel, today you are going into battle against your enemies. Do not be fainthearted or afraid; do not be terrified or give way to panic before them.' Then the officers shall add, 'Is any man afraid or fainthearted? Let him go home so that his brothers will not become disheartened too'"* (Deuteronomy 20:2,3,8).

Some who were once part of a faith community have become **deserters.** Jesus alluded to these people when He presented the parable of the seeds:

> *Those along the path are the ones who hear, and then the devil comes and takes away the word from their hearts, so that they* ***cannot believe*** *and be saved. Those on the rock are the ones who receive the word with joy when they hear it, but they have no root. They believe for a while, but in the time of testing they* ***fall away****. The seed that fell among thorns stands for those who hear, but as they go on their way they are choked by life's worries, riches and pleasures, and they* ***do not mature*** (Luke 8:12-14, emphasis added).

Perhaps these individuals who are unable to bear fruit have been a part of your congregation because they enjoyed the friendliness, the choir, the teaching. When trials, testing, or temptation proved too difficult for them, however, they walked away.

8. The only course of action for soldiers in this spiritual war is to maintain a **warrior heart**. Right relationships can spur believers on to increasing love, courage, and service for their Lord (see Hebrews 10:24,25). Wrong relationships can deter His people from the valor and courage required to accomplish His purposes through them. Courage and valor are as highly esteemed in the Bible as they are in Israel today. The Israeli military leaders of today are the ones whose wisdom and courage have won previous skirmishes as they *led*, not sent, their men into battle.

   How often in the Scriptures God commends people of valor and courage!

   > *"You need to persevere so that when you have done the will of God, you will receive what he has promised. For in just a very little while, 'He who is coming will come and will not delay. But my righteous one will live by faith. And if he shrinks back, I will not be pleased with him'"* (Hebrews 10:36-38).

   *"The wicked man flees though no one pursues, but the righteous are as bold as a lion"* (Proverbs 28:1).

   *"When they saw the courage of Peter and John and realized that they were unschooled, ordinary men, they were astonished and they took note that these men had been with Jesus"* (Acts 4:13).

   Notice how biblical men of courage attracted one another. First Samuel 14 illustrates Jonathan's courage for the Lord at Micmash: *"Jonathan said to his young armor-bearer, 'Come, let's go over to the outpost of those uncircumcised fellows. Perhaps the Lord will act in our behalf. Nothing can hinder the Lord from saving, whether by many or by few'"* (v. 6). The same courageous regard for God's honor is displayed by David against Goliath: *"David said to the Philistine, 'You come against me with sword and spear and javelin, but I come against you in the name of the Lord Almighty, the God of the armies of Israel, whom you have defied'"* (1 Samuel 17:45).

   From the time they first met, these two valiant men were drawn to each other: *"And Jonathan had David reaffirm his oath out of love for him, because he loved him as he loved himself"* (1 Samuel 20:17). Their courage produced a wonderful devotion, eulogized by David: *"I grieve for you, Jonathan my brother; you were very dear to me. Your love for me was wonderful, more wonderful than that of women"* (1 Samuel 1:26).

People who are courageous for God inspire others to be courageous. Second Samuel 23 describes the "men of valor" who joined David:

> *These are the names of David's mighty men: Josheb-Basshebeth, a Tahkemonite, was chief of the Three; he raised his spear against eight hundred men, whom he killed in one encounter. Next to him was Eleazar son of Dodai the Ahohite. As one of the three mighty men, he was with David when they taunted the Philistines gathered at Pas Dammim for battle. Then the men of Israel retreated, but he stood his ground and struck down the Philistines till his hand grew tired and froze to the sword. The Lord brought about a great victory that day. The troops returned to Eleazar, but only to strip the dead. Next to him was Shammah son of Agee the Hararite. When the Philistines banded together at a place where there was a field full of lentils, Israel's troops fled from them. But Shammah took his stand in the middle of the field. He defended it and struck the Philistines down, and the Lord brought about a great victory* (2 Samuel 23:8-12).

These three were joined by thirty other mighty men who also embodied courage beyond the average. Who are the ones in your life whom you can count on to come alongside you to stand firm in God's mighty power when trials and spiritual battles assail you? Who will "stand in the gap" (see Ezekiel 22:30) for you when the tides of sorrow or temptation threaten to loose your spiritual moorings?

Consider the neighborhood home fellowship of today in light of the early Church: Righteousness produces boldness. Think of the importance of courage. Valiant people attract other people of courage. Do you believe that your close relationships in the faith reflect you? If so, look honestly at yourself and those to whom you are close. Do these relationships exhibit the abiding presence of Jesus? Is He producing His fruit in and through each of you?

(Ponder the vine and branches relationship of John 15:1-17.) The writer to the Hebrews describes how courage and encouragement can keep followers of Jesus from sin's trap:

> *But Christ is faithful as a son over God's house. And we are his house, if we* ***hold on to our courage*** *and the hope of which we boast. See to it, brothers, that none of you has a sinful, unbelieving heart that turns away from the living God. But* ***encourage one another daily****, as long as it is called Today, so that none of you may be hardened by sin's deceitfulness. We have come to share in Christ if we hold firmly till the end the confidence we had at first* (Hebrews 3:6,12-14, emphasis added).

9. A spiritual battle can be won when the righteous courageously band together in their faith communities to concentrate their efforts. Recognize that in areas where God calls for commitment, Satan brings about dissolution of both responsibility and intimacy. One way he accomplishes this is by involving believers in a myriad of unrelated church activities.

   Another tactic is his manipulation of those he has taken captive in your faith community who continually drain you and distract you from God's real objective. You can spot these people because they never seem to have any victory in their lives. They continually complain and grumble, never able to see beyond their own needs.

   When Jesus sent the disciples out, He concentrated their effort and told them whom to engage: *"Calling the Twelve to him, he sent them out two by two and gave them* ***authority over evil spirits****"* (Mark 6:7, emphasis added); *"After this the Lord appointed seventy-two others and sent them two by two ahead of him to every town and place where he was about to go....The seventy-two returned with joy and said, 'Lord, even the* ***demons submit to us in your name****'"* (Luke 10:1,17, emphasis added). Concentration of prayer effort and assurance of your authority in Jesus routs the enemy. Satan knows that he and his minions must submit to God's people in the name of Jesus.

The current level of uncoordinated activity in so many faith communities brings to mind a poster Mike saw in the Navy. The poster was designed as a reminder to keep focused on the objective. Whatever was started was to be seen through until completion. The poster showed a man being eaten by alligators. The caption stated: "When you are knee deep in alligators is not the time to remember you were going to drain the swamp."

Can it be that the Church is knee-deep in demons because we forgot to take the offense and concentrate our prayer efforts in Jesus' name to evict the spirits that oppose us? How many people in churches today can report: *"Lord, even the demons submit to us in your name"*? Let's appropriate the power of a life submitted to God, believing that His authority can free us from spiritual hindrances and enable us to go forward to share the gospel in triumph!

10. After the ascension of Jesus into heaven, His followers gathered together for **concentrated prayer**: *"They all joined together constantly in prayer, along with the women and Mary the mother of Jesus, and with his brothers"* (Acts 1:14). The fruit of prayer concentration was 3,000 converts in one day! (See Acts 2:41.)

    To pray effectively, followers of Christ must remain in His righteousness: *"Therefore confess your sins to each other and pray for each other so that you may be healed. The prayer of a righteous man is powerful and effective"* (James 5:16). Do not wage war only to lose because your prayers were ineffective due to *individual or communal sins*. The Hebraic early Church understood that the whole nation of Israel could not stand up against the city of Ai because of the sin of one man, Achan (see Joshua 7). They remembered what God had done to Ananias and Sapphira for trying to deceive the Holy Spirit (see Acts 5).

    Victory begins with the assurance that those alongside you in prayer are in fellowship with God. There is no fellowship with one another if you have no fellowship with Him: *"We proclaim to you what we have seen and heard, so that you also may have fellowship with us. And our fellowship is with the Father and with his Son, Jesus Christ"* (1 John 1:3). If your fellowship with God has been ruptured, you have a way back to restoration: *"If we confess our sins, he is faithful and just and will forgive us our sins and purify us from all unrighteousness"* (1 John 1:9). *Unrepentance* in your faith community is like an army going into battle *without ammunition.*

11. Participation with God in His purposes requires **humble cooperation**: *"'Has not my hand made all these things, and so they came into being?' declares the Lord. 'This is the one I esteem: he who is humble and contrite in spirit, and trembles at my word'"* (Isaiah 66:2).

    *"Each of you should look not only to your own interests, but also to the interests of others"* (Philippians 2:4).

    *"For by the grace given me I say to every one of you: Do not think of yourself more highly than you ought, but rather think of yourself with sober judgment, in accordance with the measure of faith God has given you"* (Romans 12:3).

    People who cooperate together in battle share a special sense of camaraderie. It is derived from a humble, dead-to-one's-self attitude that war produces. Such selfless regard is seen in the unconscious sacrifice made by a soldier when he willingly jumps on a hand grenade in a foxhole in order to save his friends: *"Greater love has no one than this, that he lay down his life for his friends"* (John 15:13).

    The gifts of the Spirit come with the power of the Holy Spirit to carry them out. As you are trained in their corporate use in the war against Satan, something wonderful happens. The very nature of Jesus becomes produced in you. Your appreciation for the sacrifice of Jesus becomes more deeply embedded in your heart. Your regard and esteem for other believers grows. The devotion that Jesus calls for blooms in the midst of the battle:

*Jesus replied: 'Love the Lord your God with all your heart and with all your soul and with all your mind.' This is the first and greatest commandment. And the second is like it: 'Love your neighbor as yourself.' All the Law and the Prophets hang on these two commandments* (Matthew 22:37-40).

## Feedback and Testimony

We appreciate feedback based on your experiences as you use this booklet. With your permission we would like to use your testimony to inform and encourage others through our newsletter and home page on the Internet. Our address is at the front of this booklet. Thank you for bringing to life the words on these pages through personal application.

**RESTORATION MINISTRIES**

***Equipping the Church to Go Back for Its Future***

## *There's a Movement throughout the World to Restore the Foundational Principles of the Early Church. Why Now? Because God Keeps His Promises!*

It hasn't gone unnoticed in the last fifty years that God is fulfilling His promises to the Jewish people as He restores them to Israel. *"Therefore say: 'This is what the Sovereign LORD says: "I will gather you from the nations and bring you back from the countries where you have been scattered, and I will give you back the land of Israel again"'"*(Ezekiel 11:17).

Through His compassionate mercy, the Lord is also restoring the Hebraic foundations of the early Church. Jesus the Messiah came in the fullness of time *"to give his people the knowledge of salvation through the forgiveness of their sins, because of the tender mercy of our God, by which the rising sun will come to us from heaven"* (Luke 1:77,78). Now, in conjunction with the "tender mercy of our God" to the Jewish people, He is restoring the Hebraic foundations to a Gentile Church around the world.

Who is the Father recruiting to join Him in His restoration? Everyday people who will permit Him to shine through them: Jesus said, *"'I thank you, Father, Lord of heaven and earth, that you concealed these things from the sophisticated and educated and revealed them to ordinary folks'"* (Matthew 11:25, *Jewish New Testament* by Dr. David H. Stern, pp.15,16).

### *The Purpose of Restoration Ministries*

*"Repent, then, and turn to God, so that your sins may be wiped out, that times of refreshing may come from the Lord, and that he may send the Christ, who has been appointed for you—even Jesus. He must remain in heaven until the time comes for God to restore everything, as he promised long ago through his holy prophets" (Acts 3:19-21).*

### 1. Awareness

Proclaiming through written word and instruction the Hebraic foundations of thought and practice upon which the early Church was built.

### 2. Equipping

Assisting God's people in living out the restorative truths so that His purposes may be fulfilled in and through them.

Each of the books and training materials produced by Restoration Ministries is one segment of a *family of information* related to the restoration. Each publication is designed to stand alone and to equip the followers of Jesus to apply these truths and principles to their lives. The strength of each publication is found in both its content and its interrelationship to the other facets of the restoration.

## *The Hebraic Priorities of the Early Church*

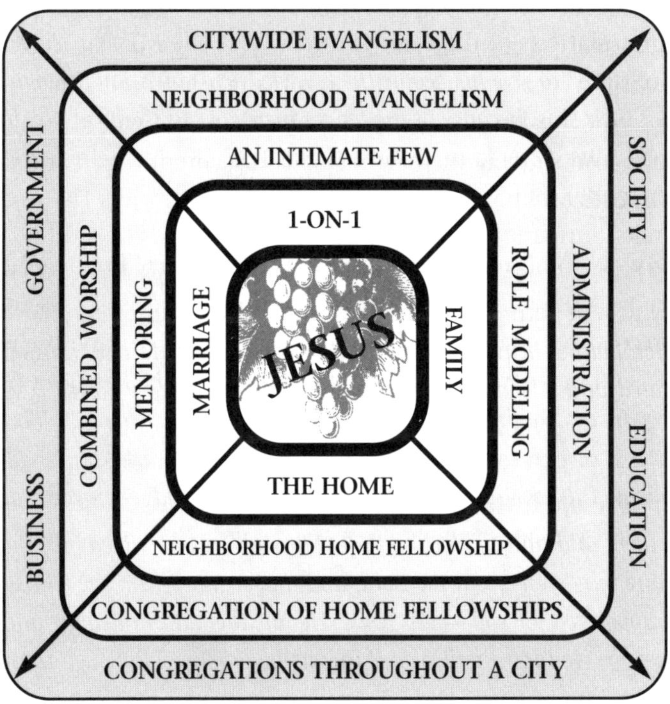

The diagram represents the Hebraic priorities of the early Church. These priorities begin with Jesus at the center and flow out from there.

## PRIORITY #1 — JESUS AND YOU

A biblically Hebraic understanding of your relationship with Jesus as a *pilgrimage* begins with the day you lovingly put your full trust and reliance in Him as Lord of your life. The publications of Restoration Ministries are worthless to you without the centrality of a Spirit-empowered loving trust in Jesus as the focus of your life.

***Please stop and pray!*** *Establish a foundation of loving trust in Jesus Christ and assurance in His Gospel before you read on.*

## PRIORITY #2 — YOUR HOME

A. **Marriage** — The essence of a Hebraic-Christian marriage of the early Church could be, *"If you want to know the extent of my relationship with Jesus Christ, look for it in the love He has given me for my spouse."* Marital love is a visible representation of a couple's relationship with Jesus. God has designed a husband to draw strength from his wife, his nurturing companion and suitable life partner, to complement him as they follow God's purposes and plans together.

B. **Family** — God is restoring the *home* as the primary building block for Christian growth within the family. The Jewish believers of the early Church recognized that their relationship with their Lord and the relationships in their homes were inseparably linked: *"Love the Lord your God with all your heart and with all your soul and with all your strength. These commandments that I give you today are to be upon your hearts. Impress them on your children. Talk about them when you sit at home and when you walk along the road, when you lie down and when you get up"* (Deuteronomy 6:5-7).

## PRIORITY #3 — YOUR HOME FELLOWSHIP

God is reestablishing a key element of the early Church: the home fellowship as an *extension of the home* for spiritual growth and supportive relationships. The earliest believers met in homes with glad and sincere hearts to break bread and to *"spur one another on toward love and good deeds"* (Hebrews 10:24).

Home fellowships are a seven-day-a-week commitment to one another to uphold righteousness and to develop increasingly supportive relationships that point each one toward greater dependency on God. Within this environment of sacrificial, load-bearing relationships, older men are taking their rightful place as shepherds, representing the Father's caring concern for His flock. These men are mentors and role models who have lived a life for Christ and can guide those younger in their walk with the Lord.

.The nation of Israel's ability to respond to God's purposes was based on their relational progression from individual, to family, to clan, to the twelve tribes that comprised the nation. At each relational level elders shepherded the people, guiding them with courage and wisdom.

Following this pattern, the Church is built on the individual, family, home fellowship, congregation, and congregations throughout a city (and ultimately worldwide). The ultimate outpouring of this relational model into their city will enable congregations to impact their society, education system, business spheres, and government.

### The Jewish People

God has promised great blessing to those who bless the seed of Abraham, the Jewish people. Over 80% of His promises to the Jews regarding their restoration to Israel have already been fulfilled. When God pours out on them a *"spirit of grace and supplication"* (Zechariah 12:10), they will be cleansed and will see Jesus the Messiah as Lord.

The Gentile Christian community must remember Paul's warning: *"I do not want you to be ignorant of this mystery, brothers, so that you may not be conceited: Israel has experienced a hardening in part until the full number of the Gentiles has come in"* (Romans 11:25). Gentile believers can pray, and through humility, work to undo the past injustices carried out by the Church against the Jewish people.

**Hebraic Practices of the Early Church**

*"I will bend Judah as I bend my bow and fill it with Ephraim. I will raise up your sons, O Zion, against your sons, O Greece, and make you like a warrior's sword"* (Zechariah 9:13).

Throughout the world the Lord is sending forth a Hebraic spirit to undo the Greek philosophical spirit that has held the Gentile Christian Church captive for centuries. By the third century the teachings and influences of converted Greek philosophers attempted to reconcile Plato and Christianity, replacing the Hebraic foundations that had strengthened the early Church.

Paul warned the Church against forsaking their trusting and obedient relationship with the Lord of life: *"See to it that no one takes you captive through hollow and deceptive philosophy, which depends on human tradition and the basic principles of this world rather than on Christ"* (Colossians 2:8).

Many of the so-called doctrines that now divide God's children are a result of the infiltration of Greek philosophy. These man-made doctrines have divided the Church for centuries. The doctrines of Jesus are understood by what His followers are willing to die for, not despise and kill others over. The Hebraic outlook also focused on personal obedience and trust in God's sovereign intervention: *"All of us who are mature should take such a view of things. And if on some point you think differently, that too God will make clear to you. Only let us live up to what we have already attained"* (Philippians 3:15,16).

# *Living Out God's Word*

## A Hebraic-Greek Comparison

### *Hebraic*

Active—appeals to the heart

**Process Oriented**

- Stresses direct participation
- Emphasizes age and wisdom
- Role modeling, mentoring, and discipleship indispensable
- Leadership by personal example
- Character of leader essential
- Personal relationships imperative

**Biblical Application**

- Doers of the Word
- Bible—reality that must be confronted
- Goal—to develop Christlikeness

**Ministry Activity**

- Small intimate groups
- Leader as facilitator
- Cooperative, participatory planning
- Spiritual gifts shared
- Frequent scheduled and unscheduled gatherings

**Fruit**

- Love, acceptance, forgiveness
- Transparency encouraged
- Active participation
- "How you serve" vital
- Each believer trained to serve
- Produces mature believers

### *Greek*

Cognitive—appeals to the intellect

**Program Oriented**

- Heavy program prominence
- Emphasizes education
- Relies on speaking skills, oratory, programmed materials, information conveyance
- Leader's personal life immaterial
- Personal relationships optional

**Biblical Application**

- Belief without personal cost
- Bible—data that must be taught
- Focus on rules—do's and don'ts
- Emphasizes distinct denominations

**Ministry Activity**

- Large impersonal groups
- Leader-directed and controlled
- Organizational roles important
- Acquisition of knowledge emphasized
- Reliance on scheduled gatherings

**Fruit**

- Mutual toleration
- Transparency discouraged
- Passivity and lethargy
- "What you know" vital
- Trained professionals utilized
- Produces spectators

Mike Dowgiewicz, president of *Restoration Ministries,* and his wife Sue administrated a church retreat center where for ten years they taught over 5,000 people from a variety of churches and denominations. While at the center, Mike was a counselor to church leaders throughout southern New England. Their ministry was recognized by the Associated Press in an article that was published nationally. Mike also was featured in an article in *New England Church Life,* "Who Pastors the Pastor?"

Before his retreat center ministry, Mike was a career officer in the Navy, having served on three deployments to Vietnam as a helicopter pilot. While he was in the Navy he gave his life to Jesus. Sue made that same commitment a few months later. Mike and Sue reside in Colorado Springs, Colorado. They have one son, Sean Michael. Restoration Ministries has its basis in research they did while living in Israel for three months during 1993-94. Through Restoration Ministries they are now sharing God's re-establishment of the priorities that strengthened the early Christians.

Mike holds a B.A. in Economics from the University of Connecticut, an MBA from California Lutheran College, and a Master of Religious Education from Gordon-Conwell Theological Seminary. Sue holds a B.S. in Education from the University of Connecticut.

## Other Resources by Mike and Sue Dowgiewicz

### *Restoring the Early Church*
A comprehensive book highlighting the Hebraic foundations of the early Church that magnified its intimacy and power. Many practical ideas for relational home gatherings. 372 pp.

### *Prodigal Church*
A 36-page narrative condensation highlighting the important points of *Restoring the Early Church.*

### *Demolishing Strongholds*
A personalized workbook to help you identify the seven basic needs God has created in you. Helps you to recognize and combat the destructive forces of demonic strongholds that keep you from fulfilling your needs His way. 66 pp.

### *Growing Relationships Through Confrontation*
An equipping workbook for individuals, families, and small groups to incorporate the Hebraic method of resolving interpersonal differences. 39 pp.

### *God's Instruments for War*
**Discovering and Coordinating Spiritual Gifts as Weapons of Warfare**

A workbook to acquaint you with the interrelational element of the Spirit's power given to all followers of Jesus so that you can effectively wage the war Satan has declared against you. Includes survey of spiritual gifts. 80 pp.

### *Christian Halakhahs*
**Loving Jesus Through the Way You Apply His Word**

This booklet articulates the Hebraic process of applying God's Word to different areas of your life, such as enacting authority in your home, educating your children, budgeting your finances, and a host of other areas. 41 pp.

### *Mishpachah Yeshua* (The Family of Jesus)
This monthly teaching newsletter supplies equipping information on the different Hebraic facets being restored in the Church today.

### *Pastoring by Elders*
A preparation guide for mature men whom the Father is recruiting to biblically shepherd and serve His people. 159 pp.

These resources are available through your local Christian bookstore

TO ORDER, CALL: 1-888-229-3041